THE UP SIDE OF DOWNS

Enjoy!

Lisa Palermo Matto

LISA PALERMO MATTO

For Dave, Casey, and Marlee,

who make my life a perfect party of four.

Love and gratitude to...

Rosalind Palermo Stevenson, my dear cousin and
kindred spirit, who guided me through the process
ever so gently with her wisdom and love.

Brooke Stratton, who brought every chapter to
life with her beautiful illustrations.

Annette Hogan, who kept my words in line with
her fearless editing.

Steve Donella and Mike Matto, who
weeded through the initial rough drafts.

Stacy Kinsella, who encouraged me to
tell Marlee's stories.

Tracy Bates, Lou Lou Delmarsh, Allison Donella,
Vicki Donella, Anne Palermo, and Art Palermo, who
made sure my I's were dotted and my T's were crossed.

Our dear family and friends, who have always been a
source of unconditional support.

The teachers, aides, administrators, and staff in the
Fayetteville Manlius School District, who embraced,
championed, and elevated Marlee.

The neighborhood, who always
looked out for Marlee. (And still does.)

And to my mother, who always encouraged me to
write. Although you are not physically here, I have
sensed your presence throughout this entire journey.
You continue to guide, inspire, and love us all.

This one's for you Betty.

FOREWORD

There was no indication of any physical or medical abnormalities. We had chosen not to have a screening test or amniocentesis prior to her birth. Ultrasound visits were my go-to appointments. It was so exciting to witness her progression and development. I brought my father to an ultrasound when I was in my third trimester. His reaction was pure joy as he marveled at the images on the screen. A healthy, active, baby girl. Four weeks later, our daughter arrived. Marlee was born with Down syndrome. This was a surprise to our family. I was only thirty-four years old.

When we came home from the hospital, we were greeted with bright, pink balloons strapped to our mailbox. All week there were deliveries of beautifully wrapped gifts, as well as a multitude of cards that were elaborately decorated with glittering stars, vivid flowers, and tiny ballerina slippers. The handwritten notes inside brought me comfort and joy.

A feeling of normalcy, I thought, after a couple of unsettling days in the hospital.

"No!" I cried in disbelief, as I opened a card from the pile.

"What's the matter?" my husband called from the top of the stairs.

"Look at this card," I replied.

It was a sympathy card. A card draped with sorrow and grief. I can still recall the dull, blue flowers and melancholy message. There was no handwritten note to fill up the depressing, blank space. Just a signature next to the word, love. Someone we knew considered the birth of our daughter sorrowful, because she had Down syndrome. That was a shock to our family. She was only 5 days old.

This is not a book about Down Syndrome. It offers no advice on how to parent a child with special needs. It is simply a collection of stories that are funny, heartwarming, and true. The vignettes shared here in no way diminish, or erase, the hardships and heartaches that we have also experienced. Like all parents, we have run the gamut of emotions raising both of our children.

One of my favorite TV series of all time is Everybody Loves Raymond. Growing up Italian-American, I can relate to the Romano family and the show's ethnic undertones. In the episode, Robbie's Wedding, Ray gave a best man's speech for his brother that really hit home with me. He notes in his speech how life is a series of ups and downs. He compares these ups and downs to photos captured on a camera. Some are bad and some are good.

"At the end of the day," he says, "you don't have to keep all the pictures…just the good ones."

That is what this book represents. Snippets of our life with Marlee. The good ones.

1

Pedicurist's Premonition

"Nice polish on those nails. The color really pops. Did you just have a manicure?"

"Sure did," I replied, admiring my hands.

"Here's the nail polish remover and a cotton ball. Take it off before we leave this room."

Did you know that during medical procedures doctors and nurses monitor fingernails and toenails? It is one of the best spots on the body to measure oxygen levels in your blood, as well as circulation. Wearing nail polish to a medical procedure is a no-no. It not only impedes the ability to monitor oxygen levels and circulation, but also inhibits the performance of the pulse oximeter that is clipped to your finger to keep tabs on the oxygen saturation of your blood. I remembered this information as I was trying to hoist myself into a pedicure chair at thirty-four weeks pregnant. The process had been explained to me a few years back when my tonsils were removed. It was one more thing the nurse had to take care of before she wheeled me into the operating room. I imagine she often had to invoke the polish removal rule. I considered not going through with the pedicure, but once I settled in the chair, there was no turning back.

The color will be expunged from my nails in two weeks if

the due date is correct, I thought, but after working so hard to get in that chair, I decided to go for it.

The pedicurist was a seasoned professional. I could tell by the way she assessed the calluses on my feet. She immediately discarded the foot file and pumice stone and began to search for something in the bottom drawer of her pedicure table. A smile came to her face as she pulled out the "big cheese" of nail instruments. It was the Microplane foot file. Most pedicure customers, including myself, refer to it simply as the cheese grater. It was uncanny how it looked exactly like the tin graters my Italian grandmothers would use to shred a brick of Parmigiana. She reminded me of a Samurai warrior reaching for a sword as she pulled it out of the drawer. It was at this point that she struck up a conversation with me. First came the standard pleasantries,

"Where do you live?

How long have you been married?

Is this your first child?"

I answered them all knowing THE question was coming. People just couldn't help themselves. When they see an expectant mother about to give birth, they do one of two things.

1. Touch the stomach

2. Inquire about the sex of the baby.

I had gone thirty-four weeks without disclosing whether this precious bundle would be a boy or a girl. No gender reveal party with Facebook live-streaming the family's reaction. No pink or blue balloons emerging from inconspicuous boxes scattered across the kitchen. No biting into cupcakes to see what color frosting had been infused into the cake. I had gone thirty-four weeks without saying a word to anyone, until now.

In addition to our soon-to-be 4 year old boy, Casey, we were going to have a baby girl. Getting pregnant had not been easy. Twelve years of Catholic school had me thinking I would become pregnant just thinking about sex. Not the case. Casey's conception was a team effort between me, the husband, the doctor, and the irrigation of my fallopian tubes. He emerged sunny side up after sixteen hours of labor. I blew every blood vessel in my face. Two miscarriages followed the birth of Casey. I was certain we were not going to become pregnant, and then we were blessed with Marlee.

Marlee Grace. Mar for my best friend Mary, her Godmother. Lee for Lisa, after my name. And Grace, for Mary's mother, who died from breast cancer. Marlee Grace Matto. Her name flowed perfectly off the tongue. I decided to tell the Foot Samurai that I was going to have a girl. A gender reveal, right there in the middle of the salon. She immediately stopped what she was doing and looked up at me.

"Million-dollar family," she said. "A boy and a girl. You got the million-dollar family."

Something about that moment struck me. I remember

thinking: yes, yes I do have the million dollar family. But there was something else. Something in her words. I couldn't quite put my finger on it, but it made me uneasy. A premonition?

2

It's All in the Delivery

Marlee was born one week early. The sporadic contractions began during Casey's 4-year-old birthday party. She hadn't even arrived yet and was already stealing his thunder.

With Pitocin flowing and all monitoring gadgets in place, we were ready for action. Contractions came and went. Then, it was time. Marlee would arrive sunny side up, just like her brother, but this time there was a moment of panic. My blood pressure dropped to a level that had doctors and nurses running into the room. Along with the dip in my pressure, Marlee's heart rate dropped significantly. When she finally arrived, she was quiet. That scared me. I remember that just as I asked why she wasn't crying, she finally let out a loud roar.

"Congratulations, you have a beautiful daughter." Marlee Grace Matto. The grandparents were right outside the door with my husband, Dave, and I could hear happy chatter in the hallway. "Mission accomplished," I grinned. The million-dollar family was now complete. Not only had I given birth to our daughter, she was the only granddaughter on my side of the family. I could hear my mother excitedly saying, "It's a girl!" The doctor had left the room for a few minutes and then returned with a worried face. He called Dave back into the room from the hallway and spoke to us in a hushed tone.

"I think that your daughter has Down syndrome," he said.

I remember slow blinking, trying to absorb what
he had just said.

I remember Dave saying, "Are you joking, doc?"

But the words tumbled out of his mouth again.

"Your daughter has Down syndrome."

And just like that, sadness drifted from the delivery room
and spilled into the hallway. The mood shifted from
laughter to tears. Our daughter had a syndrome. What did
this mean? Of course, no one said the right thing. No one
even had words. There was no chapter for this in any of the
baby books I read. The sonogram had insinuated everything
was perfect. During one of the appointments I had even
inquired about the baby's neck. Another premonition?
Maybe. Children with Down Syndrome usually have
an extra fold of skin on the back of the neck along with
heart problems. The technician pointed out there was no
extra fold of skin on the neck and the heart was healthy
and strong.

"No worries here," she said with a wink.

That night, after everyone left, it was just Marlee and me.
I examined every inch of her. Her ten little fingers and
ten little toes were perfect. She had beautiful, fuzzy, light
brown hair and deep-set hazel eyes. Her lips were pink and
pouty. Her cheeks were chubby with a tinge of crimson.

Her skin tone was a soft shade of ivory. It was smooth and unblemished. She looked like a beautiful, porcelain doll. As she began to acquaint herself with her new surroundings, her eyes appeared to sparkle, revealing her innocence and kindness. Even as a newborn it was obvious, she possessed goodness and grace. When Dave's sister Sarah arrived from Cape Cod the following day, she noticed something deep and sensitive about Marlee's eyes.

"She has an old soul," Sarah said. "You can see in her eyes that she is already wise."

How wonderful to be wise, to analyze and interpret things. Wisdom lights up a person's face, softening its harshness. Ecclesiastes 8:1 New Living Translation.

After Marlee had her bath and was examined one more time, they brought her to my room. She did not make a peep the entire evening until I put her in the bassinet. Hospital bassinets were on carts with shelves and wheels. Each baby had their own ride that the nurses would roll to and from the mother's room. The moment I set Marlee in the bassinette, she began to cry uncontrollably. I checked for all the triggers that would make a baby cry.

Was she wet? No.

Was she hungry? No.

Was she uncomfortable? I didn't know.

Breaking hospital protocol, I took her out of the bassinet and put her in bed with me. As long as she was next to me, she did not cry.

One good thing about the Down diagnosis was that the intrusive, non-medical staff did not bother us. The perky hospital photographer was a no-show. The local paper's birth announcer was a no-show. And, thankfully, the lactation consultant was a no-show. I tried breastfeeding with Casey, and I remember the woman being a bully.

She told me, "Only selfish women don't breastfeed their babies."

Then she informed me that my baby would not be as healthy if I bottle fed. I have spoken to so many women over the years who were pressured to breastfeed by the lactation consultant and family members. On top of being exhausted and unsure of myself as a mother, I also felt like a failure because breastfeeding, for me, was not a special bonding experience. In fact, it did the opposite. Once I switched Casey to the bottle, everything was bliss. I was not going to make that mistake again. I bonded with Marlee immediately and both my children have been extremely healthy. Breast feeding is a personal choice and no new mother should ever be ambushed by lactation consultants or family members when deciding what is best for their baby. If breastfeeding works for you and your baby, terrific. If a bottle is best for you and your baby, then that is terrific, too.

In the first few weeks after Marlee was born, there was not a lot of time to feel sorry for myself. One of the nurses found it odd that I was not crying and asked me about it. I reminded her that I had a healthy baby.

"What is there to cry about?" I asked.

But to be honest, I broke down a lot in those first few months. It was usually in the car or the shower where no one else would hear. The tears were not about Marlee or my love for her. They were about the unknown.

I would think, what will our lives be like with a child whose special needs did not meet the typical expectations?

My father retired from his job a few weeks before Marlee was born. I found out later that when Dave had gone into the hospital hallway and delivered the news about Marlee's condition, he had taken it the worst.

Dave said that while both grandmothers started to cry, my father pressed his head against the wall saying, "no - no," over and over.

This broke my heart. I could not imagine my father in such a state. His anguish was not just for the baby but for the life he thought we would have because she had Down syndrome. My father came over every day for a month after we brought Marlee home from the hospital. He would hold her and stay with her when I took Casey to and from nursery school. It got to the point where Marlee would look for him in the morning. As soon as he would arrive, she would go right to him. While I was grateful for the help, I was more impressed with how my father committed to connecting with his granddaughter. He was the first one in our extended family that made it his mission to form a special bond with this baby.

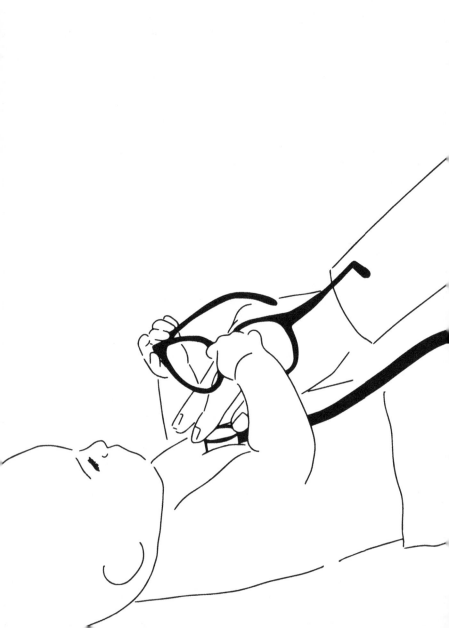

3

Down Playing It

Marlee did not have the classic symptoms and difficulties that can be common with the diagnosis. Oh, you could tell she had Down syndrome by her facial features sometimes, but nothing was overly pronounced. She had passed the exam at the pediatric heart specialist with flying colors. She had no physical issues whatsoever. Our family pediatrician said she was perfect and the therapists from early intervention were amazed by her strength and attention span. Low muscle tone is a common symptom. There was no sign of it. When the doctor was listening to her heart during her two-month appointment, Marlee ripped the stethoscope out of her hands and then knocked the glasses off her face. As a parent who had still not fully come to terms with the diagnosis, I was beginning to think maybe she didn't really have this syndrome they call Down's.

Maybe they were wrong, I thought. Maybe she will grow out of it. Or, maybe a miracle will happen, and that extra chromosome will disappear.

But when I would start to believe a miracle had happened, something would always jolt me back to reality, like the time I brought her on a trip to the toy store before her first Christmas.

An unkempt looking man walked up to us and said, "I got a

brother that's one of those."

Shocked and not sure how to respond I replied, "How nice."

Instances like this would happen every so often, but they did not provoke my anger. Instead, these unfortunate occasions motivated me to become steadfast in making sure Marlee would grow up to be able to handle herself, as well as any hurtful words that might come her way.

4

Don't Believe Everything You Read

I had chosen not to dig too deep when it came to gathering information regarding the development of children with Down syndrome. From my limited research, I did discover that these children were not expected to hit developmental milestones as promptly as typical kids. Although this information was disappointing, it did not frustrate me. Our pediatrician gave us information regarding a family centered program for infants and children between the ages of newborn and three years old. The Early Intervention Program provides services to work with children who have developmental delays or were diagnosed with a condition with a high probability for delays. I was unaware that such a program existed until Marlee was born. Eligibility for the child is determined through an evaluation process and services are based upon a child's individual needs. Speech, physical, and occupational therapy sessions were in place for Marlee before she was one month old. The therapy sessions took place in our home and our entire family was encouraged to participate alongside Marlee. Twice a week two therapists from the Early Intervention Team would work with Marlee on achieving set goals and evaluating her progress. From day one of interacting with Marlee, the therapists were impressed with her cognitive and motor abilities. Trying to negotiate all the moving parts of having a child with a developmental diagnosis would have been very difficult without these amazing women. They did not just provide a professional service, they genuinely cared for Marlee and our family. They counseled us with any questions we had regarding the therapy, Marlee, or the unknown future. One of the greatest things they did was provide Dave and me with a constant stream of inspiration and hope. It was incredible to watch them work with Marlee to master rolling, crawling, walking, thinking, learning, and problem solving. They were a priceless support system, always positive and focused when it came to Marlee making her developmental marks. Because I was fortunate to have these two women in my life, I did not feel the need to reach out to local support groups. That didn't matter, though, because somehow they found me. I received a call from one of the many support groups in our area. As the woman began to give me information regarding the group, she asked,

"How is your baby's health?"

I replied that she was great with no medical setbacks or heart issues. I reiterated that Marlee was happy and healthy and that we were extremely blessed.

You can imagine my confusion when she replied, "Well, she's healthy now."

"Sorry?" was all I could muster for a response.

"Well, she may be healthy now, but that won't last."

As she continued to relay words of discouragement,

I remember the anger I felt. This was a person in a position to offer support and assistance. Instead, she offered pessimism and bitterness. All I wanted to do was get her off the phone. I was not ready to join any group at this point, but this one would definitely not be on either my short or long list. I know there are fabulous chapters of groups and associations that assist parents and families with positive guidance and love, unfortunately, this was not my experience. Even though I could dismiss the caller as someone who was bitter and cynical, it still hurt to hear her pessimistic take on children with developmental needs.

When Marlee was one week old we were invited to dinner at a friend's house. It was casual attire, so of course I picked out a leopard print skirt, black top, tights, and a matching leopard print hat for her to wear.

During cocktail hour I overheard our host say to the hostess, "That baby doesn't look any different than any other kid I've ever seen."

I loved that he thought that and that he said it. My sentiment exactly. And that is how we chose to raise Marlee.

There was no disparity with developmental marks in the first three years. She smiled at one month, held her head up while lying on her tummy at two months, and rolled from back to tummy to back at five months. She was walking by thirteen months and potty trained by the time she was 3 years old. The only delay we noticed seemed to be with her speech. I prayed so hard for her to be able to talk. She finally started putting words together at twenty-eight months and has not stopped talking since. Soon, I began to pray that she would stop talking. Even when she sleeps, she has full blown conversations throughout the night.

The only major setbacks we had regarding Marlee's disability were with strangers, like the man in the toy store, who would make ignorant comments. The only thing that exposed her disability as a baby and toddler were her facial features. At the time, this really bothered me. I considered having plastic surgery for her during those first three years. There was a renowned doctor at Strong Memorial Hospital in Rochester who specialized in "normalizing" the pronounced features that most children with Down syndrome inherit. The surgeon would build up the bridge of the nose, which is characteristically flat in children with Down syndrome, as well as modifying the shape around the eyes. After taking Marlee to three appointments, I was over it. If people looked at her and only saw a kid with a disability, that was their problem.

5

The Hood

We moved into our "forever" home on Monday, July 2, 2001. That night was the official start of the July Fourth holiday. Because everyone had the next two days off from work, the neighborhood was hosting a block party. Talk about great timing. The action took place right outside our front door. We couldn't have asked for a warmer welcome, with food, drinks, games, music, and fireworks. It reminded me of the Fourth of July scene from the movie, The Sandlot. Parents congregated around the food and drink tables, while the kids were running and playing. Dave carried Marlee in a backpack, where she slept soundly right through the fireworks. The neighborhood may have only been ten years old, but it had a 1950s or 60s kind of vibe.

During the summer, the kids in our neighborhood would gather together every morning. They would play all day, every day, into the wee hours of the night. They played classic games like Kick the Can and Ghosts in the Graveyard, as well as hours and hours of football. Nothing was organized. Parents did not facilitate and micromanage. Unless someone was bleeding or unconscious, they needed to figure things out for themselves. Old and young, syndrome and non-syndrome, they all played together. They spent hours zigzagging through each other's backyards. Every day was a new adventure.

One of Marlee's favorite things to do when she was little was to sit in the passenger seat of Casey's motorized jeep. She loved to ride with him as he drove all over the yard and driveway. Marlee was included in most of the neighborhood games right from the get-go. She went from being a passenger in the jeep to taking the wheel herself. She would swing for hours in the backyard and serenade the neighbors with songs from the Sound of Music and Hey Jude by the Beatles. Our next-door neighbor made a game out of trying to guess the name of the song. Because her speech was delayed, it was difficult to understand her words. Guessing the song was not an easy thing to do. He would have to listen carefully before giving a final answer.

When Casey was ten years old, he got a handheld video camera for Christmas. He began to record family celebrations, as well as action skits with the kids from the neighborhood. One of my favorite videos he made was a remake of the opening to The Mary Tyler Moore Show. He called it, Marlee Tyler Moore, and he gave his sister the starring role. He had Marlee recreate each scene and matched it with the music. He filmed her working the typewriter, smelling a bouquet of flowers, driving a car, and imitating the iconic shot of Mary tossing her hat into the air.

It kept them busy for hours. Casey and his neighborhood buddies would spend their summer days making movies. Everyone was included. One of the neighborhood boys who was a few years younger than Casey was a master at editing. He would make the kids retake scenes and manage the recording. He would add music, scenery, sound effects, even digital animation. The movies were well done for a bunch of pre-teen amateurs.

Some communities form a committee to create a Neighborhood Watch. Our neighborhood had a Marlee Watch. No committee needed. Instinctively, the neighborhood watched out for Marlee. Sometimes she would leave the house without a trace. These incidents were known as unauthorized jail breaks. She has taken years off my life with these escapades. Her disappearances were legendary in the neighborhood. Whenever she was suddenly unaccounted for, everyone would leap into action.

The first time we were unable to account for her whereabouts, she was 4 years old. I was in the kitchen making her lunch when she just disappeared. I couldn't find her anywhere inside the house, so I began to comb the neighborhood. Other neighbors jumped in to help with the search. After twenty minutes with no sign of her, I called the police. This would not be the first time we would need their assistance in locating her. While talking to the officer, I couldn't help but notice the way the neighbor's dog was looking at me.

Chelsea was a yellow Labrador Retriever. She belonged to the family next door and her owners were not home. They had left the garage door open just enough for Chelsea to fit underneath, allowing her to go in and out. I had checked their house first, figuring Marlee had gone over to see Chelsea. They were pals. Marlee would give Chelsea makeovers using colored chalk. Chelsea would sit, wagging her tail, while Marlee applied streaks of blue and red doodles all over her furry face. Chelsea was a hero in our house. She had protected Marlee from a stray dog that ran into our yard while Marlee was on the swings. Chelsea had run through the electric fence in order to fend off the intruder. Since then, Marlee would visit Chelsea at least once a day.

There was something about the way Chelsea looked at me that made me go over to her. It was almost like she wanted to tell me something. Chelsea greeted me as I walked up the driveway. She kept looking at the garage. Without even thinking, I knelt on the asphalt and slid inside. I immediately became upset because Marlee was not there. I was about to crawl back outside when Chelsea came in. She stood at the door, which led to the house, and began to scratch at it. Jeff and Linda always kept that entrance locked. The only reason I tried to open it was because Chelsea wanted to go inside. To my surprise, the door was unlocked. I let myself and Chelsea inside. Upon entry, I discovered one of Marlee's shoes in the mudroom, and one on the kitchen floor. When I did not locate her on the first floor, I proceeded upstairs to the bedrooms. I found her in the corner of the youngest child's room. She had taken all the picture books off the shelf and was leafing through them.

I was so relieved to find her safe. I scooped her up from the floor and took her outside where the police officer and other neighbors were waiting. Everyone breathed a sigh of relief. Chelsea followed. She assumed her position in the driveway, where Marlee gave her a hug goodbye.

The Marlee Watch was always ready to spring into action. Sometimes their service was rendered before we even knew there was a problem. This was the case one morning, before the sun had a chance to rise. Most mornings, Marlee would wake up before the rest of us. She would turn on the television and watch cartoons. Occasionally, she would have other ideas. On one such morning, our neighbor Steve left his house very early to drive down state for a sales meeting. As he drove past our house, he noticed the garage door going up and down, quickly and erratically. He knew something wasn't right and decided to reverse his course so he could investigate. He found Marlee sitting in the front seat of Dave's car playing with the garage remote. Steve told Marlee to go back in the house and back into bed. He watched as she padded her way up the driveway and into the house. When she was safe inside, he shut the garage, locked Dave's car, and hid the keys.

6

Who's on First?

No matter what kind of locks or alarms we purchased to secure the doors or windows, Marlee always found a way to break free. She would sneak out undetected and then slip back in effortlessly. When Marlee was six years old, she infiltrated the neighbor's house across the street. The Donella family, Steve, Vicki, Allison, and Nathan, moved into the neighborhood exactly five weeks after us. Marlee was eight months old and their youngest, Ian, was not yet born. Through the years, they have become family to us. It is no surprise that many of the stories recounted here include them.

On this particular day, Vicki was upstairs in the shower while the rest of her family was out running errands. We know Marlee left our house. We know Marlee entered the Donella's house. We know what took place in the Donella's house happened while Vicki was in the shower and Steve was out with the kids. We have no idea how long Marlee was in the house or how long Vicki was in the shower. We do know that when Steve and the kids first got back home, Marlee was not there, and nothing seemed out of place. None of us would have known she was ever there if it was not for one crucial piece of evidence. What was the evidence you ask? A message left inadvertently on the answering machine. When Steve returned with the kids, he spotted the blinking red light, beckoning him to push play. A recorded message on an answering machine is like opening a box of chocolates. You never know what you are going to get. It could be good news; it could be bad. When Steve pressed play, the message did not disappoint. Marlee took a call from Steve's dad while she was roaming around in their house. His dad thought he was speaking to his 3-year-old grandson, Ian. She must have not answered until the machine triggered the recording process. The conversation that was recorded with Steve's dad, otherwise known as Grampy, sounded like a skit from Abbott and Costello's famous, Who's on First routine.

As we still have the recording, we were able to transcribe the call exactly as it happened.

Grandpa D: "Is this Ian? This is Grampy."

Marlee: "Oh, hi."

Grandpa D: "How you doing?"

Marlee: "Good. How you do?"

Grandpa D: "Are you getting ready for tomorrow?"

Marlee: "What?"

Grandpa D: "Are you playing golf tomorrow with me?"

Marlee: "Me?"

Grandpa D: "Yea!"

Marlee: "Who? Who you again?"

Grandpa D: "Is this Ian?"

Marlee: "No, not Ian.

"I'm Ma Maddo."

"Marnee Maddow, Marnee"

Grandpa D: Laughing

Marlee: "Mawnee Maddow

Grandpa D: "Is your daddy there?"

Marlee: "My daddy? Um, no. He not here. He home."

Grandpa D: "He's home?"

Marlee: "Yea."

Grandpa D: "Can I talk to him?"

Marlee: "No, he's home."

Grandpa D: "Then can I talk to him?"

Marlee: "No! He home!"

Grandpa D: "OK. I'll call back later."

We still have the recording and we still laugh just as hard when we hear it today, as we did all those years ago.

7

The Set Up

Steve Donella and Marlee have always had a special connection. They are both a little cheeky, speak their minds, and love a good prank. Kindred spirits, one might say. We have had a weekly card night with Steve and Vicki Donella for years. Our game of choice is Pitch. Whether it is just the four of us or another couple joins, Steve and I are always partners. These matches usually take place on a Friday night. We either make pizzas or order out with the kids, and then deal up the cards after dinner. On one such occasion it was the Friday before Halloween and it was our turn to host. We invited another family from the neighborhood to join and had just finished with dinner. Diane and Jerry Hart lived next to the Donellas and had a son the same age as Casey. While the kids were occupied in the basement, we took our seats and began to play. Marlee decided basement shenanigans with the boys were not for her, so she retreated into the office to play games on the computer. Before we had a chance to finish our first game, she rushed into the kitchen with a terrified look on her face. She told us that someone was outside the window looking in at her. We reassured her that she was safe.

"It's probably the jack-o-lantern we carved for Halloween," Dave said.

But she didn't agree with that explanation. After several minutes of protest, she prodded her buddy Steve to leave the card table. He agreed to go to the office with her and investigate. As he peered through the window, it was hard to make anything out because it was so dark. Upon further review, he noticed there was something directly underneath the window. Using the light from his phone, he discovered the item in question was Marlee's Barbie doll. The doll looked eerily wretched, sprawled face down in the dirt.

"There's no one there," Steve said. "It's just your doll. Do you want me to get it for you, Marlee?"

"Yes, please," was Marlee's quick response.

The office was on the first floor, so the rescue should have been easy. As Steve opened the window to retrieve Barbie, he noticed the screen had been pushed out on the bottom. Then he noticed the start of a mischievous smile take over Marlee's face. Before he could he reach out the window to scoop up the doll, Marlee tried to push him out. Not with a dainty little push, but with a cross-check to the back. He was half hanging out of the window when she tried to finish the job by lifting his foot. Steve reclaimed his balance and the Barbie at the same time. Instead of screaming from fear, we now heard the two of them screaming with laughter. She got him and she got him good. It was premeditated. It was deliberate. And it was genius. She was sending a message. She had thrown the gauntlet and would now wait for Steve's next move. Down syndrome or not, Steve would not let her get away with this. That is what I love about Steve and all our friends in the neighborhood. They treat Marlee just like they treat any other kid on the block. Her days were numbered and she couldn't wait to see how Steve was going to strike back.

8

Operation Marlee

Senior trips have become a rite of passage for many high school students. East Coast teens often spend their senior-year spring break at all-inclusive resorts in Mexico and the Caribbean. Casey and his buddies planned for a week on Singer Island in Florida. While most teenage boys would opt to be as far away from their parents as possible, this group was encouraging us to spend the week somewhere nearby. The boys had been together since elementary school and we loved all of them, as well as their families. Dave and I wanted to make this time with Casey special as he would be leaving for college in the fall. We planned a staycation for Marlee with her favorite sitters. She was looking forward to the activities we had planned with each of them while we would be away. It took months to coordinate.

We had decided to drive to Florida. We took Marlee to school the Friday before Spring Break, and from there started the tedious trek south. Ordinarily, I would have felt uneasy that we had not dropped Marlee directly to her sitter, but the schedule I had devised left no room for error. I had painstakingly plotted each piece of the puzzle. If everyone followed the plan, Marlee would seamlessly transition to each destination without a hitch. The least complicated piece to this puzzle should have been the school pickup. This was Vicki Donella's assignment. Easy peasy. The school knew Vicki was coming. Marlee knew Vicki was coming. And Marlee's aide knew Vicki was coming. The school would not let a child leave with anyone other than a parent or guardian, unless it was cleared ahead of time. Vicki had been cleared. What could go wrong? Traffic. Traffic is what could and did go wrong. Vicki was unable to make it to school on time for pickup because of congestion on the highway. Makes sense in hindsight. It was the Friday before Spring Break. Everyone was trying to sneak out a little early. She called her husband, Steve, to see if he would be able to get to Marlee on time. "No problem," he said, "I will leave work now." He arrived at the student pick up lane and began to inch his way forward with all the other cars. When he finally rounded the circle by the door, he eyed Marlee standing with her aide. Perfect, Steve thought, there she is.

Steve pulled up, rolled down the window, and said, "OK Marlee, time to get in."

He didn't introduce himself or bother to explain about Vicki's predicament. He was focused. He had a job to do and he was all business. He knew if he messed up my timetable, he would be in big trouble, so he was direct and to the point.

Once again, he said, "OK Marlee, time to get in."

Marlee gave Steve an impish grin, and then she looked at her aide.

"Who you?" she shouted.

48

"Marlee," Steve replied, "that's not funny!"

The aide looked confused and the line of cars behind him was growing. He explained to the aide that Vicki was his wife, and that an unforeseen problem had occurred that prevented her from doing the pickup.

"Here," he said. "Here is my license. See, I'm a Donella too. Really." He gave the aide a wink and said, "Marlee, let's go!"

This time, Marlee not only responded with a "who you?" but she ran behind her aide and cowered. Sweat was forming above Steve's brow.

"Marlee, get in this car now," Steve said. "If we mess this up, I am going to be forced to call your mother, and she is not going to be happy with either one of us. And I, for one, do not want to make your mother mad."

The mom card worked. Marlee came out from behind her aide. "Oh, Steve," she said laughing, "here I come. I just joking."

Thankfully, another teacher was there who could vouch for Steve, and the first step of Operation Marlee was a success.

9

Rain - Rain Go Away

Summertime in our neighborhood meant kids were outside from morning until night. They would start to congregate outside of someone's house and have a plan for the rest of the day. Marlee would try to keep up with Casey and the rest of the gang as best she could. She loved being outside. She would set up picnic lunches on the lawn, lay by the pool, and play with her Barbie dolls in the driveway for hours. Even if it rained, she would grab her little pink umbrella and continue to play.

Marlee had an uncanny knack of predicting when it was going to rain. There were days when the sun was shining bright and she would say, "It's going to rain Mommy."

I would look to see if there were any clouds and say, "Not today, Marlee."

But she was always right. Was she sensitive to the change in the barometric pressure or did she have a special gift? The girl was more reliable than a meteorologist. As long as there was no thunder, Marlee had no problems. Thunder would send Marlee into hiding. She would become desperately frightened and hide in the bathroom. There was nothing we could do to help except to wait out the storm.

When Marlee was in fourth grade, something happened

during outdoor gym class that would expand these fears. Whatever happened caused Marlee to not only fear thunder, but to also be frightened of clouds. This fear would last for years. From what we could piece together, the class had been playing kickball when a cluster of dark clouds blocked out the sun. Marlee heard a classmate say the word storm, and without thinking, ran as fast as she could back inside the school. At first, no one could find her. She was hiding in a bathroom stall. For Marlee, it was her safe place, no windows. She was insulated from the crashing sound of thunder and bolts of lightning, just like her bathroom at home. From that day on, if there was one cloud in the sky, Marlee would not go outside for gym or any other outdoor activity. It didn't matter if there was only one. It didn't matter if it was white, fluffy, and shaped like a puppy. She would retreat indoors for the day.

This fear was paralyzing for her and our family. We tried medication, which seemed to alleviate some of the anxiety, but it did not take away the fear. We had her work with a children's therapist. She loved the Barbie dolls the therapist used to initiate conversation, but the sessions did not help. Nothing seemed to work. The times I felt the saddest for her would be when the pool was packed with the neighborhood kids. She would stay inside and watch the fun from her bedroom window. There was nothing we could do to help her overcome her worry. She would need to conquer this on her own. And eventually she did. The desire to be with friends was her ultimate motivation. Marlee learned to dig deep and push through her fear. She would stay out when it was cloudy for as long as she could before disappearing into the house. She would wait a few minutes and then try again. And again. And again. She was resilient. She learned to cope with her anxious feeling. She has even been able to stop taking the medication she was prescribed for the anxiety. She can still sense the rain before it arrives, but she is no longer afraid.

10

The Zoo

The light of summer begins to fade in mid-August for Upstate New York. As fall emerges from summer's shadow, it casts a cool splendor over the landscape. There is a subtle shift in temperature as the air readies itself to embrace the cold. A contrast in scenery is underway. Fiery oranges mingle with glitzy golds and ruby reds. This collision of colors is reflected on ripened leaves and berries. Autumn in New York delights the senses and inspires the soul.

I awoke to the sunlight illuminating the sky. It was going to be a picture-perfect autumn day. The schools were closed to commemorate Columbus Day, so I decided to do something special with Marlee. A trip to the apple orchard was the obvious choice.

But on a day like today, I thought, every other parent would be thinking the same thing. "It would be an absolute zoo at the apple orchard," I said to nobody.

As soon as I said the word zoo, I knew where to go. The zoo would be the perfect place. It would not be as crowded as the apple orchard. I called my friend Lou Lou to see if she, and her son Ben, would like to join us. Ben and Marlee had been friends since they were two years old. I met Lou Lou, and her daughter Lily, at the school playground just before Casey began kindergarten. We were both trying to familiarize the kids with the school. The minute we started talking, I knew we would become good friends. We were both Italian, loved to cook, and wore big hoop earrings. If that wasn't enough, Lou Lou had an incredible sense of humor. Lily and Casey started kindergarten together. Meeting each other on the playground was meant to be. Our families have been the closest of friends ever since.

At the time of this outing, Ben and Marlee were ten years old. We were all looking forward to seeing the animals and exhibits. It was not crowded at all. I had made the right decision. After wandering around the complex, we finally came to the elephants. The Rosamond Gifford Zoo in Syracuse has since built an impressive wildlife preserve for elephants as well as many other animals. It is truly a remarkable place to visit with over 43 acres of land that is home to more than 700 animals. The elephant enclosure was a more intimate setting during this visit. Guests of the zoo could stand at the fence of the exhibit, and watch the elephants interact with each other. Zoo patrons, young and old, couldn't wait to see these gentle giants. You were even allowed to pat their trunks as they walked by the fence. The elephants were the most beloved and revered animals at the zoo. Lou Lou and I found a bench by the fence, where we waited for the elephants to arrive.

As Lou Lou and I chatted, we noticed a mother with five children in tow. The kids were so well behaved. They moved in a line from oldest to youngest without holding hands. The ages seemed to range somewhere between fifteen years to a toddler. We marveled at the way the children interacted with each other and gave huge kudos to the mom. In hindsight, I should have known such impeccable behavior from someone else's children would open the door for Marlee to wreak havoc. When the elephants came out from the indoor part of the enclosure, everyone in the area ran to position themselves in front of the fence. Ben and Marlee landed next to the five siblings. All eyes were on these majestic creatures. The trainers worked with the elephants before they guided them to the fence. Everyone wanted a turn to gently stroke their ears and trunk. While Ben and Marlee waited in line, Lou Lou and I began to collect our belongings from the bench. The elephant enclosure was right by the exit door, so we would leave as soon as they had their turn. Ben returned to the bench after petting the elephants, but Marlee was not with him.

"Where's Mar?" Lou asked.

Before Ben could answer, I spotted Marlee running towards the exit door.

"Oh, Geez," I yelled, and started to run after her. "Marlee," I shouted. "Stop!"

She must have known I meant business because she stopped dead in her tracks. It was when she turned to look at me, I realized she was holding the toddler from the family with five kids. It was at this point that words a little stronger and more colorful came out of my mouth. Amazingly, no one from the family had noticed their littlest member was gone. They were still at the fence trying to get the elephants to come back towards them. I yelled to Lou Lou and pointed towards Marlee. Without saying a word, Lou Lou made her way to the fence, and struck up a conversation with the mom. She kept her occupied while I carefully took the little girl from Marlee's arms. I sprinted towards the family, placing her back in line with her siblings. She never made a peep.

When we got back to the car, Lou Lou asked Marlee why she picked up the baby and ran.

Marlee said, "Because she so cute and I want sister."

Marlee was right, she was adorable. No wonder she wanted to take her home. We did not return to the zoo for a long time. Although the incident had alarmed me, I also made an important discovery. I realized that the mother of five, whom I had deemed infallible, wasn't perfect either. When her child had gone missing, she, along with the other four kids, hadn't noticed. She was a mom, just like me. Perfectly imperfect. Just trying to get through each day without losing it. "It" being your sanity, patience, or even your kid. Most moms and dads are just trying to do their best to raise good humans. We should always remember to give ourselves and each other a break.

11

Life is a Cabaret

The television series House premiered in 2004 and lasted eight seasons. In 2014, Casey discovered the series on Netflix and became hooked. Hugh Laurie played the main character, Dr. Gregory House. Casey was fascinated with the story lines and binge watched the episodes. I assumed he was interested in the medical aspect of the show. Perhaps he was considering a career in medicine. Wrong. The focus for Casey had not been the medical storylines. He was fascinated with the way Laurie portrayed Dr. House as brilliant, but quirky. He had many flaws. The most obvious shortcoming depicted by the character was popping the narcotic Vicodin to help manage pain he endured due to a leg injury. Because of this, Dr. House was forced to use a cane to help him walk. Laurie's use of the cane caught Casey's attention. So much so that he purchased a cane for himself. Nothing fancy. Just an everyday walking stick from the drug store. Casey has always been the comedian in the family. His humor is dry and quick. He can impersonate anyone. The cane became a fixture in our house for months. Casey brought it to school under the ruse he was injured. He had been given permission to use the elevator and classmates carried his books. This lasted for three days until a teacher uncovered the truth and put a stop to it. Casey kept the cane safely locked in his room, so that Marlee couldn't take it. I didn't give the cane much thought, until Casey announced it was missing.

"I'm sure it will turn up soon," I told him as he left for school. "I will help you look."

We looked everywhere when Casey returned from school. We searched all through the house, the yard, the car, the garage, and nothing. Marlee was not home. She had been picked up after school by her Community Habilitation Aide, Mrs. Rice. Twice a week, Mrs. Rice would escort Marlee to stores, restaurants, and the library. She would assist Marlee in navigating each setting, and to reach her specified goals. The focus of community habilitation is to strengthen life skills for individuals with disabilities. The skills are designed to fit the individual's needs. Once a goal is mastered, skills are reevaluated, and new objectives are added to the plan. At the time, Marlee's goals consisted of understanding stranger danger and following traffic rules. Mrs. Rice also worked with Marlee to improve her confidence in social situations. She helped her develop appropriate dialogue when speaking to the librarian, food servers, or store clerks. About an hour before Marlee was due back home, Lou Lou and my other dear friend, Tracy, showed up unexpectedly at my front door.

"What's up girls?" I said.

"Well," said Lou Lou, "we just left Kohl's department store, and you'll never guess who we ran into?"

"Who?" I replied.

"Marlee!" They both said laughing.

Oh no, I thought, why are they laughing?

Lou Lou explained how she had been at the customer service desk making a return. While she was waiting for the transaction to be completed, both she and Tracy heard a sound coming from one of the aisles.

Tracy said that it sounded like, "a one-legged pirate stomping his way through the store." As the intermittent thumping became louder, Tracy noticed Marlee rounding the corner carrying a cane. "She was slanted to one side leaning on the cane like Mr. Peanut."

When Marlee noticed Tracy, she then began to twirl the cane and dance. A mini Liza Minelli, right there in Kohl's.

"Marlee," said Tracy, "how are you? You look amazing today. Is that your cane? Where did you learn those dance moves?"

"Who you?" Marlee yelled. "Don't talk to me. I don't like you."

Before Mrs. Rice could react to Marlee being rude, Lou Lou stepped in. She had also witnessed the interaction and did not appreciate the impolite and disrespectful way Marlee had treated our good friend Tracy.

"Excuse me," said Lou Lou. "Did I just hear you being rude to Miss Tracy? I do not appreciate that kind of behavior from you and neither will your mother when I tell her about this."

"I sorry, Lou Lou," Marlee answered.
"Don't tell my mom. Love you both."

And with that, Marlee planted a kiss on both Lou Lou and Tracy, did an about face with her cane, and twirled out of the store with Mrs. Rice.

I love that our family, friends, and neighbors always treat Marlee the same as they would their own child. They are willing to call her and Casey out when I am not around, and vice versa with their children. It takes a village to raise our children and that makes me so thankful for where I live.

Oh, and the cane. How did Marlee break into Casey's room and sneak it out of our house? How did she sneak it into school, and then into the store with Mrs. Rice? To be honest, after the surprise visit from Lou Lou and Tracy, I completely forgot to investigate. The good news was that it came back, and it wasn't broken.

Sometimes it's best to leave well enough alone.

12

Gone Fishing

Luxury for some people equates to expensive jewelry or fancy cars. For moms of young children, having the house to yourself is a luxury. This kind of indulgence was a rarity, but when it occurred, I savored every second. One Saturday morning, I returned from grocery shopping to find the house empty. The stillness was delicious. Dave had left a note that he and the kids were running errands. It would be years before I learned of the unfortunate series of events that took place. Events that still cannot be explained. What we do know is that Marlee had some type of interaction or altercation with a group of fish.

Instead of running errands, Dave pulled a "pop in" on our friends Tom and Stacy. There was no Ring doorbell camera to prevent the "pop in" back then. Once you answered the door, it was all over. The kids were all similar in age. Their son Jack and our son Casey were good buddies, their daughter Marley and Marlee were in the same grade, and their daughter Max was somewhere in between. Dave had a system when he traveled solo with the kids. He would arrive at a destination, let the kids loose, and completely lose track of them. He became legendary for this.

Dave and Tom tuned into a football game while the boys played outside, and the girls watched a movie in the basement. When Stacy went to check on the kids, she found the boys still outside, her girls still downstairs, but Marlee had disappeared. It was not unusual for her to leave a room unnoticed. She was quick. She was quiet. And she could slip out without being detected.

Not wanting to panic anyone, Stacy began checking all the rooms in the house. Basement was clear and so was the first floor. She made her way up the stairs and began sweeping the bedrooms. Master was clear and so was Jack's room. It was at this point that she could hear a splashing noise coming out of Max's room. When Stacy opened the door, she could hardly believe her eyes. Max's aquarium, which had housed hundreds of tiny painted stones, a tiny treasure chest, a tiny cave, and four brightly colored fish, was empty. The water was still in there, well most of the water, but everything else was scattered across the bedroom floor. Stacy could see Marlee on the floor under Max's bed. She was sopping wet.

"Marlee," said Stacy. "What did you do?"

"Who you?" replied Marlee as she picked painted pebbles from her hair.

 "Who am I? You know who I am," said Stacy. "Where are the fish? Why is your hair wet?"

"What fish?"

"Max's Fish."

"Who's Max?"

Stacy began to scour the room in search of the fish. Maybe, she thought, just maybe they are still alive. But there was not a fish to be found. Not a trace. Not a scale. Not a fin. Not a clue.

Stacy brought Marlee into the bathroom and helped her pick the aquarium pebbles out of her hair. She blew her hair dry and put her back down in the basement with the girls. She never said a word to Dave about what happened. He finished watching the game, scooped up the kids, and came home. It would be years before she shared the tale of Max's fish with us.

Stacy choosing to keep this to herself speaks volumes about her as a person and a friend. She knew how upset I would have been to learn Marlee had caused such a commotion.

The mystery of what took place on the day of the "pop in" has never been solved. What happened to the fish?

Some of the theories people have floated over the years are:

Marlee flushed the fish.

Marlee ate the fish.

Marlee hid the fish.

One thing is certain. The fish never saw it coming.

13

It's Better in the Bahamas

We had six pieces of luggage to check at the gate between
the four of us. Each passenger was allotted two checked
bags plus a carry on. No charge. All free. The year was 2008
and the motto fly the friendly skies still rang true. Five
of the bags contained food, and one kept our clothes. No
kidding. We were going to Treasure Cay Island. A narrow
slice of heaven connected to the Abaco Islands in the
Bahamas. We had rented a beautiful condo from friends
that was only steps away from the white, sandy beach. The
bags we checked contained precious cargo. Inside each
piece were meals I had prepared ahead of the trip. We had
lasagna, pasta, sauce, meatballs, steaks, chicken, a seven-
pound baked ham, hamburgers, hot dogs, cereal, coffee,
creamer, snacks, and rolls. Anything that wasn't a liquid,
or what the airlines considered an illegal vegetable, was
fair game. Each item was frozen and wrapped up tight.
The airplane baggage compartment was cold, so we knew
the food would remain frozen while we traveled. The TSA
in Syracuse threatened to confiscate my lasagna for their
lunch. Thankfully, they refrained from taking it, and all the
food made it to the Bahamas intact. We were there for ten
days and went out to dinner only once.

The plane from Syracuse to Fort Lauderdale was your
regular sized jet with flight attendants, beverages, and beer

nuts. The plane from Lauderdale to the island resembled a child's toy with a wind-up propeller. I was sure the baked ham would bring down the plane. There were twelve seats total on the plane, including the pilot's. He welcomed us on board, pulled in the ladder, closed the door, and revved up the engine. No flight attendants, peanuts, or emergency instructions on this flight. Smoking was apparently permitted for the pilot, who lit up a cigarette right before take-off. There was no curtain or wall to separate him from the rest of us. When he needed to relay a message, he just shouted over his shoulder. Fear seemed to grip the face of every passenger except one, Marlee. As the plane began to ascend, bouncing from cloud to cloud, she squealed with delight. When the plane would take a dip due to an air pocket, she would scream, "Whee!" There were times she would even hold up her arms like she was riding on a rollercoaster.

The airport in Abaco was tiny. We collected our bags quickly and found a driver to transport us to the condo. The island was pristine. The ocean revealed deep shades of emerald, turquoise, and teal. The water shimmered in the sunlight. We marveled at the treasures found on the beach. Sun-bleached sand dollars, multicolored conch shells, and an array of starfish trying to conceal their existence beneath the sand.

While we were walking back to the condo from the beach, Marlee made a run for the pool. Her head start did not worry me as I could see inside the gate. In the few minutes it took me to rendezvous with her, Marlee had already made friends. There was a crew of twenty family members from Buffalo, New York. They had taken over the entire pool. Two of the dads had set up a human launching pad in the shallow end. The kids formed a line in the water and the dads would take turns tossing them into the deep end. They would chant the name of each child three times before releasing them into the air. The laughter was infectious. Marlee did not want to be left out. She jumped in the pool and got in line.

When it was her turn, I heard them chant, "Marlee, Marlee, Marlee."

It only took a couple of days on the Island for Dave and me to completely unwind. The weather had been perfect. On our second day walking the beach, we noticed a tiny island. The tide was so far out that we could almost reach it by walking. We decided to check it out before the tide turned. When we no longer touched the sandy bottom with our feet, we began to swim, towing Marlee on a boogie board. The island was basically a gigantic rock, but the kids had fun exploring it. On the third day, Casey found a starfish washed up on the beach that was bigger than his head. It was still pink. I had no idea they grew so big.

As we tucked the kids in for bed that night I thought, this place is an absolute paradise.

I should have known better than to think something like that. The calm we had been granted was to ready us for a storm. I had just unwittingly invited trouble into paradise.

73

Means of transportation while on Treasure Cay consisted
of walking, riding bikes, and using a golf cart. We were
fortunate to have access to the golf cart and bikes through
the owners of the condo. One evening after dinner, we
decided to go out for ice cream. The four of us hopped in
the golf cart and made our way to the local stand. After
enjoying our treats, Casey and I decided to walk back to
the condo. We wanted to take a detour and stroll the beach.
We waved goodbye to Dave and Marlee, who were already
in the golf cart ready to leave. When Casey and I returned
to the condo, the cart, along with Marlee and Dave, were
nowhere to be found.

Where are they, I wondered? It was getting late.

Eventually, I heard the cart make its approach, and swing
around the back of the condo. The two of them quietly
climbed the stairs to the deck. I could tell by the panicked
look in Dave's eyes that something had happened.

 "You better sit down for this one," he said. And breathing
heavily he explained what had transpired. "Marlee
and I were in the golf cart on our way home, he said.
"We drove by a couple we recognized as part of the
group from Buffalo."

"OK," I replied.

"Well," he said, "I stopped the cart to talk with them. Marlee
was still eating her ice cream cone, so I got out and left her
in the cart alone and continued talking."

"Oh Geez," I murmured.

"The husband and I were talking about football and the Buffalo Bills. His wife noticed Marlee was sitting alone and decided to climb into the cart and keep her company. I didn't notice that Marlee had moved onto the driver's side," he said.

"Oh no," I replied, lowering my face into my hands.

"The wife started asking Marlee questions. She asked Marlee her name, age, and what was her favorite ice cream flavor. It was really sweet," he added. "I turned away from the cart for one second Lisa, one second, and without any warning, the cart was gone."

"What do you mean gone, Dave?" I was standing up now and shouting. "How does a cart just disappear?"

"Well, I didn't see it leave. I heard it. But I didn't actually see it leave."

"You said you took your eyes off the cart for one second. How could you not see it leave?"

"I saw it swerving unsteadily down the path that leads to the beach. I ran as fast as I could after it. The woman's arms and right leg were flailing as the cart sped on. The worst part was I could hear Marlee laughing. She thought it was funny. I knew the cart needed to stop before she crashed into something or tipped it. After what seemed like an eternity, the woman was able to grab the wheel and slam her foot on the break. When I got to the cart, it was just awful. The woman was shaking, and Marlee's ice cream had landed on one side of her face."

The woman stumbled out of the cart and ran to her husband. She was in shock.

She told him, "There had been no warning. One minute she was eating her ice cream cone, and the next she was pressing both feet on the gas pedal."

"The cart took off like a shot," Dave said indignantly. "Before I could even react, the cart was just gone. They left immediately, didn't even say goodbye."

"Didn't say goodbye? You're lucky the husband didn't punch you," I said. "I want to punch you."

"So many things could have gone wrong, the cart could have crashed or overturned. Lisa," he said, "this could have been a very serious situation."

I was about to respond to him when Marlee bounded into the room.

"Hi Daddy, fun. Don't be mad mommy. I have fun."

We tried very hard to convey just how dangerous her actions had been. What could have happened. How she could have been hurt. We wanted to make sure she never went on a joy ride like that again. But it was hard to stay upset. Marlee lives in the moment. To continue to reprimand would be stealing her joy. She was over it and so was I. I decided not to continue to be upset with Dave. I didn't want to steal his joy either.

The rest of our trip was non-eventful in Marlee terms. Dave's mom had flown over from Florida and spent a few days with us. That was fun. It gave Dave and I an opportunity to do things without the kids. When we flew home, we checked one piece of luggage and five empty bags. It really was a great trip.

In August of 2019, Hurricane Dorian wreaked havoc in the Eastern United States, Puerto Rico, Eastern Canada, and the Caribbean. One of the hardest hit places was the Abaco Islands in the Bahamas. The storm delivered winds in excess of 185 mph, causing major structural damage as well as killing a number people. We hope Abaco Islands and her people make a full recovery. We can't wait to be able to visit there again one day.

First Day of Kindergarten

Leopard outfit for first dinner party

Ian and Marlee at bus stop

Ben and Marlee at the
Rosamond Gifford Zoo's
Elephant Exhibit

4th Grade chorus members

Marlee with her aides at the 4th grade show

Marlee with her 4th grade
teacher after the show

Marlee on the school
playground in 4th grade

At the pool

In the Bahamas with the Starfish

Marlee and Casey with their cats Sal and Sam

Halloween in the neighborhood

Marlee & Kristen

Neighborhood Football Game

New Year's Eve 2013

Steve with the Barbie and Ian

14

The Florida Chronicles

Before Dave and I were married, my parents purchased a condo in West Palm Beach. It was a two bedroom, two-and-a-half bath winter oasis. An escape from the gloomy skies of Upstate New York. Syracuse is one of the snowiest cities in the world. Yes, I said world. Check it out yourself. The arctic air greets you with a one–two punch. The first hit takes away your breath. The second stings your cheeks. The snow usually makes an appearance before Halloween and can last until Mother's Day. The catch phrase, "Winter is coming," made popular by HBO's award-winning series Game of Thrones, has been an oft-heard phrase in Upstate New York for years. Our family took full advantage of my parent's condo in Florida. We would go at least once or twice between January and May. Dave and I would make the long drive in those early years no problem. When Casey was born, we began flying down. He was fifteen months old on one of those trips. As we boarded the plane, I could see some of the kidless passengers watching to see which row we had been assigned. The last thing any of them wanted was a potentially disgruntled toddler near their seat.

As we took our seats, I proclaimed, "If this baby makes a fuss and ruins your flight, I will buy you a cocktail. However, if he is an angel and doesn't make a peep, you owe me one."

I'll admit, it was a risky move. But the risk paid off. Casey was as good as gold. Before we arrived in West Palm, two beers and one vodka tonic arrived at our seats. Some of our fellow passengers made good on the deal and sent cocktails to Dave and me.

Three years later, Marlee was born. Instead of flying, we decided to make the long drive with the kids. This would allow us to bring strollers, scooters, bikes, and toys, as well as the kitchen sink. Twenty-one hours door to door. How bad could it be?

Well, it could be downright hell. Traffic jams, sick kids, detours, screaming kids, exhausted parents, rest areas, potty breaks. It was never an easy ride, but somehow we convinced ourselves to do it year after year.

When Marlee was three and a half, our trip south was made a bit more bearable. We caravanned more than half the way with the Donella Family. They traveled every year to spend a week on Florida's West Coast with Steve's parents. Our goal was to make it to Raleigh, spend one night with our old neighbors, and then go our separate ways. We were on target to do just that when things came to a screeching halt in Pennsylvania. A little snow can cause a lot of delays once you leave New York State. The highway departments in New York are well prepared with plows, salt, and manpower when the snow and ice begin to fly. Once you cross state lines, there is a noticeable difference in how roads are maintained, especially in the winter. We found ourselves stuck in one spot for over three hours due to weather conditions that would not have slowed us down back home. Thankfully, Ian was still potty training. Vicki had packed his portable potty and that little plastic toilet came in handy for all of us.

After an hour of gridlock, people began getting out of their cars and trucks to stretch and talk to folks in neighboring cars. Steve and Dave were getting out to stretch a lot. It seemed odd to me that they were not overly annoyed by the traffic delay. I'm not sure if it was me or Vicki who noticed it first. There was a Girls Gone Wild bus behind our two cars. The frequent stretches were an attempt to view what was going on inside the bus. We were only in Pennsylvania and they were already enjoying some of the perks of spring break.

Because of the delay, we had to spend the night in Virginia. We made it to our friends who lived in Raleigh the next day. It was great to catch up with them. They had only lived in the neighborhood for a year, but the friendships were solid. Our three families had spent every Friday night together, switching houses each week. After a fun night of reminiscing, we parted ways the next morning. We planned to complete the last leg of the trip on our own. As soon as we pulled into my parent's complex, I breathed a sigh of relief. My parents were waiting for us in the condo parking lot when we arrived.

We took full advantage of my parent's place and all the amenities that came with their condo. The pool was across the street. Next to the pool there was a playground, tennis courts, basketball courts, and a pond with ducks. We would spend most afternoons at the pool once the kids had finished with lunch. We made plans to take my parents for dinner midweek of our stay. Marlee and I returned from the pool early to get a head start on getting ready. After giving Marlee a bath, I sat her down in front of the television to air dry, so I could shower. I would get her dressed once I was finished.

The doors to the condo were locked, as well as the patio gate. You could not go in or out of the gate if it was locked. The gate key was hidden in the flower box. When I finished drying my hair, I called down to Marlee to let her know it was her turn. Marlee loved when I would blow dry her hair. But she did not respond. I called to her again, and nothing. I made my way down the stairs and noticed she was no longer sitting in front of the television. I didn't panic until after I checked the kitchen and bathroom. No Marlee anywhere. The main door was still locked, but when I tugged at the sliding glass door, it easily opened. Marlee had managed to unlock it. Well I thought, she must be sunning herself on the patio. When I went out on the patio my heart sank. The gate key which was supposed to be hiding in the flower box was sticking out of the lock. One of the patio chairs had been pulled up to the gate door.

"Oh my God," I screamed to no one. "She did it again."

She had found the key, climbed a chair, inserted it into the lock, and made her escape. Now I was panicked. There was no telling which way she may have gone, and I did not know any of the neighbors. I was running down the path outside of the condo when I saw her. A woman was holding her hand and walking her towards me. Marlee had not only left the condo, she was not wearing any clothes. The woman who found her was very upset. She looked at me as if I was the worst mother in the world. Then she let me have it.

"This is your daughter," she said.

"Yes," I excitedly replied.

"Mommy!" Marlee shouted.

"I found her just wandering around the complex," she said.

"I know," I replied.

"She's naked," she said.

"I know," I replied.

"She could have made her way to the busy road, fallen in the pond, or have been kidnapped," she said.

"I know," I replied, "thank you for walking her back."

And with that, she gave me one last look of disgust and stomped away.

She was right. All those things could have happened. Thank God they didn't. Thank God she was safe. And thank God my parents never found out Marlee had run away from the condo naked. They would have sold the joint on the spot.

My parents did end up selling their condo five years later. They made the decision to sell because my nephews were playing sports in the high school and they did not want to miss their games. Instead of spending the winter in Florida, they now rented during the months of March and April. They had found a place near the beach in Jupiter, and we were excited to spend spring break with them.

Marlee suffered from reoccurring ear infections. She was constantly on antibiotics and required medication during this visit. Thank goodness for urgent care facilities. Ear infections are very painful. The medicine prescribed was not the same as what her pediatrician used, but the doctor from urgent care assured me she would be feeling better within a day. And he was right. After twenty-four hours, Marlee was much better. We decided to go to the pool once her ear improved. The kids brought their beach toys and were having fun keeping each other company.

I foolishly whispered to Dave, "Perfect day, huh," when Casey emerged from the pool.

He had pulled off his goggles and was swimming towards us. He was yelling something we could not understand. It became apparent he had made a ghastly discovery while swimming.

"Marlee pooped in the pool," he screamed.

I jumped from the lounge chair without speaking, looking at him in disbelief. He screamed it again, only this time louder.

"Marlee pooped in the pool!"

Not only could I hear him, but every person in the pool and on the tennis courts could hear him too.

"Marlee pooped in the pool!"

The words ricocheted off of every object inside the pool area.

She had never done anything like that before.

"Why," I moaned.

It would be a couple days before I figured out it had been the medicine she was taking. It had caused her to have a backup of sorts. I think the warm water encouraged things to start moving again and it took her and everyone else by surprise.

Before Dave could put his book down to move, I leapt to the edge of the pool and yanked both Casey and Marlee out of the water. I whisked them back to the condo in record time. It was not nice leaving Dave there by himself. But desperate times call for desperate measures. I knew I would need to move fast before any discussion was broached about how we were going to fix this. All the other people who were lounging around the pool began scurrying off in every direction. I'm sure some were on their way to the maintenance office to file a report. I looked back once and only once. I saw Dave pacing the deck of the pool.

"That poor man," I murmured. And then I scurried away.

When Dave returned to the condo, he looked like a soldier returning from battle. He was disheveled, disoriented and confused. He explained how he submerged himself into the pool armed with only a little red shovel and a yellow plastic sand sifter. The mission had not been successful. Any attempt to retrieve the poop sent it darting like a torpedo, until it finally blew up into miniscule pieces.

"At that point," he said, "even the sifter was useless."

After aborting the operation, Dave went to the maintenance office and reported the incident himself. The woman at the desk was initially concerned that Marlee had an accident and was hurt. When she realized the accident involved an involuntary bowel movement, she was relieved. We never went back to the pool. To this day, I have nightmares of the management staff draining the pool and sending someone in to scrub the bottom, like Bill Murray's character in the movie, Caddyshack.

15

The Happiest Place on Earth

We have been very fortunate to visit both Disney World and Universal Studios. Marlee's first visit to Disney was when she was 6 years old. Dave was very worried that Marlee would have meltdowns in the park. He had inquired about using Disney's Disability Access Service Card, which would have allowed our family special access to the rides and attractions. I refused to do this. I had not yet come to terms with Marlee having mental or emotional delays. Because she was not physically handicapped, I did not think it would be right to use the pass. I was being ridiculous. Disney had implemented these passes with great sensitivity to ensure every visitor would be able to enjoy the park. It can be hard enough for children without special needs to make their way around the park. Add a sensory, physical, emotional, mental, or medical issue to the equation, and the happiest place on earth can become a hostile environment. I didn't take into consideration that Marlee had sensory issues and difficulty in transitioning from one activity to the next. The pass would have been a gift to her, as well as our family. At that time I believed if I admitted that Marlee needed special assistance, it meant I wasn't doing my job as a mother. Instead of embracing the pass, I wanted to prove I didn't need it. It was selfish and foolish on my part.

February Break is an especially busy time at the Disney

parks. Marlee did OK standing in the lines, although she did have her share of meltdowns. When this happened, she would firmly plant herself on the ground in the middle of Main Street USA. During one of these screaming tantrums, I realized I had made a grave mistake in not using the access card. I also found that most people who witnessed Marlee's collapse were incredibly supportive. They did not intrude but would instead give a sympathetic look or encouraging nod.

The park personnel who portrayed Disney characters were outstanding when it came to interacting with Marlee. Can you imagine walking around for hours in the Florida heat dressed in those costumes? I would be miserable. These lovely individuals were kind and patient with our daughter. I took note of how they would carefully approach her. They would walk slowly and make sure she was comfortable with them being near her. They would follow her lead when giving a hug or posing for a picture. At the attraction, House of Mouse, there was a long line of small children who were waiting to give Minnie Mouse a hug. Marlee patiently waited her turn without any problems. When it was time for Marlee to meet Minnie, she hugged her tight and would not let go. I made my way to Marlee and gently began to pull her away. I was afraid she was taking up too much time. Mini stopped hugging Marlee and held up her hand to me. She gave me a definitive sign that said, no worries mom, I've got this. The woman playing the part of Minnie continued to give Marlee her undivided attention. When their time together came to an end, Marlee smiled and waved goodbye. It was a good lesson for me. Sometimes, I worried so much about others, that I did not prioritize my own children's needs.

In January of 2017, we took a trip to Orlando. We had booked a five day stay at the Portofino Hotel, located on the grounds of Universal Studios. Casey was twenty and Marlee was sweet sixteen. Casey left two days ahead of us and drove Dave's mom from New York to her condo in Stuart, Florida. Grandma Rosie, as we liked to call her, was going to spend the winter there with her two sisters. Once they got to the condo in Stuart, Casey helped her unpack and spent the night. The next day, he drove her car across the state to meet the rest of us at the airport in Orlando. We had taken the JetBlue dinner flight which departed from Syracuse at 6 P.M. It was a quick, nonstop flight, and Marlee was awesome on the plane. We sat in the first row and the flight crew doted on her. Along with keeping Marlee entertained, the flight attendants provided Dave and I with free alcohol. It was an outstanding flight!

Casey was spot on with the airport pickup. He had us to the resort before 10 p.m. Universal did an exceptional job designing the hotel and surrounding area. You felt like you were in Portofino, Italy. Our room was a large suite with marble floors. The sitting room and extra bathroom were an added bonus. The staff was attentive to our needs from check-in to check-out. They gave us a tour of the hotel and grounds, told us the best time to grab breakfast and where to catch the boat to the park. They also gave us tips for restaurants and attractions. By the time we settled our things in the room, we were starving. We decided to find a place within the hotel to grab a bite. I was very worried about going to a restaurant so late at night, after the long day of traveling. Would this be overkill for Marlee? I was almost going to suggest ordering in when I decided to just let it go. We found a little Italian restaurant that was still serving and grabbed a table. That night was one of the best times we ever had as a family. The four of us were laughing, talking, and sharing what rides we wanted to go on. Marlee was involved in every aspect of the conversation. I was so glad I did not follow through on ordering room service.

Another thing I changed my mind about was using the access pass. At Universal, it is called the Attraction Assistance Pass. Even though we were visiting in mid-January, it was still jam-packed with people. The lines for many of the attractions were over an hour long. Marlee would have had a difficult time keeping it together waiting in the long lines. She had her own agenda of what she wanted to do while at Universal. She had been working very hard to manage her feelings when she felt overwhelmed or overtired. As she became busier with activities, friends, and life in general, she became aware that she needed to use calming techniques like breathing and counting to keep calm. Although she was very successful at handling her emotions most of the time, sensory overload was still a possibility. When this happened, my only course of action was to try and reason with her. When she was younger, I could physically pick her up and move to a quieter location, but this was no longer possible. We would now have to wait for her to control herself. I was very grateful to be able to have the pass for Marlee and for our entire family. It allowed us to use a special line for most rides, which cut out the wait time. Thankfully, no one seemed to mind our VIP status. We felt like celebrities. "Finally," Casey exclaimed, "My homie with an extra chromie is paying off." (Get it? People with Down syndrome have an extra chromosome in their DNA.)

The Wizarding World of Harry Potter was at the top of Marlee's agenda. We spent hours riding the Hogwarts Express, Escape from Gringotts, Harry Potter and the Forbidden Journey, and Flight of the Hippogriff. Dave almost lost it with the amount of money we spent buying wizarding attire and wands in Diagon Alley, and buttered rum drinks at the Leaky Cauldron. We went to a place called Shutterbuttons, where we were filmed acting out twelve different scenes from various Harry Potter Movies. We dressed in robes, used our wands, and gave the performance of our lives. It had been a fabulous day. No fighting or meltdowns for anyone.

The next day proved to be a bit tougher for Marlee. Exhaustion set in by midday. We had kept a fast pace trying to see and experience everything the park had to offer. The Hollywood Walk of Fame was a must see for us. Marlee absolutely loves Dean Martin. We play a lot of different music in our house and two of her favorite singers are Dean Martin and Frank Sinatra. She has a huge poster of Dean in her room, and I wanted to get a picture of her next to his star on the walk of fame. I became so intent on getting the picture, I overlooked the signs of Marlee starting to lose it. By the time we found Dean's star, she wouldn't even look at it, let alone take a picture next to it. I couldn't believe it. One picture, I pushed. We walked all over the park just to find it. She wasn't budging and neither was I. Dave and Casey were both telling me to give it up. Unfortunately for me, and everyone else in our vicinity, I didn't take the cue. I didn't let it go. I pushed once more for Marlee to have her picture taken next to Dean's star. Instead of taking a picture next to it, she dropped to the ground and laid on top of it. She began to sob uncontrollably. One of her worst breakdowns ever. People were stopping and staring. One woman asked if I needed help. Dave and Casey were frustrated with Marlee and me.

"Why did you have to keep pushing for the picture?" they said.

I was wondering that myself. Marlee had been so enchanted with Dean Martin's music and movies, that I became obsessed with capturing a photo of her by his star on Universal's Walk of Fame. I put that on the must see list, when in fact, Marlee had no interest in visiting that part of the park. There was nothing exciting to Marlee about any of the star's names engraved into the slabs of stones. I told the boys to go ahead and I would wait it out with Marlee. Once she calmed herself, we took the boat back to the hotel and called it quits for the day. Times like these would feel so disappointing in the moment. Casey was especially upset that Marlee and I had to leave. Instead of being grateful for all the good times we had so far, we were focusing on the one negative. When the boys came back from the park, we were all in a better mood. One minor setback would not define our Universal vacation!

Towards the end of our stay, Casey learned that two of his high school friends were also visiting Universal. The girls had arrived the night before and they made plans to connect. One of the girls had babysat for Marlee and wanted to see her. She offered to take Marlee out for pizza, so we could have dinner with Casey. Marlee was so excited to be with the girls, and we were excited to spend time alone with Casey. We were spending the next day in the park and then driving to Grandma Rosie's for the duration of our vacation. Casey wanted to be sure we hit up the Spider Man and the King Kong attractions. We had not made it to those rides yet and they were on his list. We got back to the hotel to find the girls watching a movie with Marlee and enjoying some ice cream. It was now Casey's turn to go out with his friends. I thanked the girls for hanging with Mar and told Casey not to be out too late. "You don't want to be too tired to enjoy your last day in the park," I said. "King Kong and Spider Man are waiting for you!"

But we woke up the next morning to find a citation slid underneath our hotel door. We would not be spending our last day at Universal together. According to the citation, Casey was banned from the park for one year.

"What the heck is this?" I said out loud. "Casey! Wake up."

It seems Casey and his friends decided to go to Universal City Walk, where there was shopping, music, restaurants, and clubs. At some point in the night, they decided to wait in line to get into one of the clubs. The problem was they were all only 20 years old, and the legal age to enter was 21. They tried to use fake IDs, which failed miserably. They did not make it past the bouncer. He took away their phony IDs and had the police escort them back to their hotels. The police copied each of their licenses and were told they would be banned from all the parks at Universal for one year. Talk about a buzz kill. Universal, as well as other major parks, use a biometric fingerprint scanner for entry. There was no chance Casey, or his friends would be allowed back until a year had passed. It was apparent we would not be able to spend the last day at the park together and it was most unfortunate for Casey as he missed out on King Kong and Spider Man.

Casey thought we would just pack up early for Grandma Rosie's and skip the last day of the park because of his situation. He was wrong. He was really upset. But this time he couldn't blame Marlee. This episode was a good reminder that we all make mistakes. Just like the mistake I made by trying to compel Marlee to have a photo op with Dean Martin's sidewalk panel. We just need to own them and move on. Marlee was an absolute gem that last day.

16

Stealing the Show

Marlee began her education at Bright Beginnings Nursery School. Bright Beginnings was considered a typical preschool program. Casey had gone there for two years and we wanted Marlee to have the same experience. The director of the program implemented provisions for her needs, including having an aide on site to assist her throughout the morning. She was the first student with Down syndrome to attend Bright Beginnings. The students didn't look at Marlee as different or handicapped, they just saw her as their classmate and friend. The aide helped Marlee navigate classroom schedules, social situations, and daily routines. It was a great experience for her and for everyone at the school.

When Marlee graduated from Bright Beginnings, one of the teachers admitted to us that she had been very nervous about having her in class.

"I didn't know what to expect," she said. "What I discovered," she continued, "was that Marlee made everyone better. We were all a little more kind, caring, and patient. We taught her, and she taught us. It was a privilege to have her in class. She made us laugh every day and taught us to appreciate life. Thank you for sharing her with us. I will never forget her."

The transition to elementary school was simple because of the skills Marlee learned in preschool. It was also helpful that most of the kids from Bright Beginnings went to the same school. They knew her and she knew them. They had already experienced being in a school setting together.

Marlee's teachers and administrators throughout her school career worked diligently to make sure her educational experience was exceptional. Marlee was able to participate in every activity the school offered. This included having a minor role in the Spring musicals. Performances would include singing, hand motions, and dancing, as well as talking parts. It was a chance for kids to showcase their artsy side for parents and grandparents. I could not imagine how much time and effort it took to make sure each kid participated in some way. Persuading them to sit still for the duration would be hard enough. I have attended school performances where kids have fallen off the stage, vomited, fainted, and made faces at the crowd. To be honest, these moments were more entertaining than the actual show. Each year the production would become a little more robust, as students embraced the opportunity to display their special talents. Marlee's fourth-grade show was a western theme. Certain students were selected to sing solos and to participate in a dance sequence. Marlee had the responsibility of walking across the stage and sprinkling sparkle dust from a bucket. I thought that was fantastic. Little did I, or anyone else, know that Marlee did not appreciate her limited role. She decided to reinvent her part and surprised everyone the evening of the performance.

The night arrived. Every fourth-grade parent, sibling, and grandparent was packed into the auditorium. The stage was set with a backdrop that resembled the old west. The costumes for the main characters were handmade and elaborate. The piano was tuned, the risers in place, and the kids who had starring roles took center stage. One of Marlee's classmates was nonverbal and used a wheelchair. His stationary role was the driver of a covered wagon. The set crew who designed the wagon attached props to his wheelchair. It was very clever. The show was about to begin, and I was nervous. I wanted Marlee to do her part and pay attention to her cues. I wanted her to do what she had rehearsed and blend in with the other 120 kids with non-starring roles. The kids without a standout part were strategically placed on the risers. Marlee was on the left side of the curtain, right in front. I was crossing my fingers that she would not make faces, throw up, or run off the stage.

During the opening scene of the show, the improvisation began. It became apparent that Marlee wanted to be part of the dance number. Thinking back, I did recall a conversation where she asked if she could wear one of the pretty costumes. I didn't pay attention because we had been sent a letter stating what should be worn. The one hundred or so "chorus" members were to wear jeans and a white tee shirt. The girls performing the dance number were dressed in ballet leotards with sparkly pink tutus. They assembled onto the stage and were waiting for their cue. As they began to glide across the floor, Marlee hopped down from the riser.

Oh, no, I thought.

She then inserted herself into their routine.

"Dear God," I moaned.

She must have been watching them during rehearsals because she was actually pretty good. No one said a word, and no one removed her from the dance number. Beads of sweat began to build on my forehead.

OK, I thought, one little detour, I can handle that.

But then I noticed something else. Whenever there was a singing part, whether group effort or soloist, a voice from beyond would belt out the words after the others finished. That voice belonged to Marlee. She would wait for the other kids to stop singing, and then sing the same line of the song. She would sing so loudly, everyone in attendance could hear. Every time this happened, I could hear laughter coming from the audience. At this point, I was praying for her to vomit, make faces, or faint. At least that would get her off the stage.

Throughout the night, her classmate in the wheelchair/ covered wagon remained in the same spot on the stage. When the storyline involved the wagon, the main characters would gather around it. But for most of the show, he and the wheelchair sat quietly in one place. This was not overlooked by Marlee. Once again, she decided to shake things up. She hopped down from the risers, walked over to the wheelchair, and took hold of the handles. She was going to show everyone what a covered wagon was supposed to do. She pushed the wheelchair from one side of the stage to the other, waving at the crowd. She parked the wheelchair front and center, right in the middle of the show. While the teachers looked panicked, I started to laugh. I loved that she did that. I loved that she wanted to show off her friend to the entire audience. It was an innate desire to do something that most people would have ignored. Her classmate playing the role of the covered wagon would have remained a stationary character for the entire production if it had not been for her. Marlee saw it as an opportunity to give someone, who otherwise would have been overlooked, a chance to shine. Many of us try to live in the now. Marlee does it naturally. She always lives her life in the present moment. She does not worry about what other people think. She knows what she wants and why she wants it. She also knows how to compromise. She didn't have the pretty costume, but she was going to join the dance number anyway. Many times, people view a child's behavior as impulsive. What I have come to appreciate about Marlee is that her conduct often encompasses the needs of others as well as herself. Pushing her friend in the covered wagon was not about bringing attention to herself, but giving him the attention he deserved. Giving him his moment on that stage. It was more than just living in the now, it was an act of pure goodness. A magical scene, unrehearsed, and from the heart. My beautiful girl delivered this to the audience effortlessly. A moment of grace.

The other parents loved it. Her final moments on stage would lead to a crescendo of laughter and confirm that she really did steal the show. The music teacher was giving shout outs to the students who had done vocal or instrumental solos. After announcing their names, a voice could be heard from the seat risers.

"Hey! What about me?"

You guessed it. It was Marlee. The teacher, not missing a beat responded.

"Thank you too, Marlee Matto!"

It brought down the house.

17

Freedom from Speech

Marlee's vocabulary could be quite colorful at times. This seemed to become pronounced when she began middle school. Middle school would be different than elementary school for Marlee. The building was much bigger and had three floors to navigate instead of just one. There would be new friends to make, as the middle school population was a combination of students from two different elementary schools. It would also be the first time Marlee would have to change classrooms for a subject. It was during this time that Marlee began to realize she was a little different from the other kids. She hated that. Even though she had aides to help her throughout the day in elementary school, the assistance was not overt because every classroom had at least one teacher's aide assigned to it. By the time she was in fourth grade, the aides allotted her much freedom. They worked very hard to ensure she could do most things in the building on her own.

The transition to middle school took time. Learning how to get around the school, as well as being assigned new teachers and aides were challenging. Switching rooms for classes was not a huge deal for Marlee. In elementary school, she would leave her classroom to go to speech, as well as occupational and physical therapy. Once she finished her scheduled therapy, she would always return to her classroom and catch up on missed work or activities. In middle school, if she had to leave a room for therapy, she would miss the lesson and not return to that class until the following day. Marlee took special education classes for math and English. She was in a typical setting for the rest of the day.

Her favorite classes in middle school were science and social studies. Like me, she enjoys hands-on learning. Her last class of the day was social studies with Mrs. Lalik. She had been one of Casey's favorite teachers when he was in middle school and Marlee loved her too. Sometimes, Marlee would have to leave a class and go to speech or one of her other therapy sessions. This is what happened one afternoon during social studies. The class was working on an activity together. Halfway through the class, Marlee was called out to go and work with her speech teacher. Sometimes her speech teacher would push into the classroom to work with her, and other times they would go to the therapy room.

The therapy sessions were part of her IEP (Individual Education Plan). An IEP is created for children who have special needs. Dave and I, along with her teachers and school administrators, would meet each year to evaluate her goals and create a plan to help her succeed in school. The IEP confirms that she will receive the support and services recommended to her plan. Many parents must fight for their children to receive services, so we appreciated all the help she received. The therapy times were scheduled to not interrupt the same class every day. Most days, Marlee did not mind going to the therapy room. It was super fun. All the therapists incorporated creative strategies like using bubbles, Barbies, and computer games to help students achieve their goals. But on this day, she did not want to leave her social studies class. She was enjoying the group activity with her classmates. We hadn't considered that Marlee may want to occasionally opt out of a service if her class was doing something special. It became an unfortunate oversight for us and the school.

Marlee's social studies class was the last period of the day. When Marlee left social studies, she was instructed to take her backpack, as she would be dismissed from school by the speech teacher. Marlee left the classroom reluctantly. She was upset she had to leave. She did not reveal her disappointment at first, and actively participated in her speech lesson. When the period ended, Marlee had to walk by her social studies classroom to line up for dismissal. The kids from her class were already in the hallway waiting to leave. It was at this point, Marlee's frustration from being pulled from class was released.

She walked by her classmates and proceeded to call each and every one of them an assortment of colorful names. The email we received from the vice principal revealed that her most popular term of endearment was a word referring to one's backside. The adjectives dumb and hole were occasionally thrown in to accentuate this word. Upon receiving this email, I began to cry. I waited for Dave to come home and showed him the message. I was sure he would be as upset and horrified too. As he began to read the message, he slowly began to chuckle. After he finished, he

113

laughed out loud. He grabbed me, gave me a hug, and said,

"Honey, I know there are things that happen that break your heart when it comes to Marlee, but this should not be one of them. All kids have their moments. And you know what, maybe next time they will let her stay in her class if she is doing something that interests and excites her."

"Wow!" I thought. Dave was right.

And truth be told, from then on, if Marlee did not want to leave a class to go to speech, occupational, or physical therapy because she was really into her lesson, she did not have to. She was becoming her own advocate. She was the one who initiated this change in her educational plan. Marlee had a voice and she was not afraid to use it.

18

The Marlee

While I blame myself for some of the colorful word choices Marlee uses, I cannot take credit for her innate ability to give the finger. The pointer finger that is. And at precisely the right moment. We call this gesture, The Marlee, and it caught all of us by surprise the first time she did it. It was to one of Casey's neighborhood buddies when they were playing football in our front yard. Marlee tried to join the game, but the boys wouldn't let her. Usually, something like this would cause her to have a meltdown, but not today. She grabbed the ball, gave them the stink eye, raised up her finger, and then threw the ball down on the ground.

This caused the boys to burst out laughing, and then they all started copying her. And not only did the boys start using their pointer finger to give The Marlee, but all the parents did too. It was not just the gesture itself, but it was how she executed it. Using the pointer finger instead of the middle finger allowed her to accurately aim it at her intended mark. Because she didn't have to worry about bending the other four fingers, it seemed effortless when she chose to fire it off. She would commence with a resolute stance that would demand your attention, her expression callous. The wrist would roll, and the hand would rise. Then, with a firm and unwavering extension of the finger, she would give you her special salute. No one was safe from being on the receiving end of it, and no one knew when their turn would come. No one, that is, except for her dad. For some reason, Marlee chose this as a parting wave when he would drop her off at middle school each morning. Dave would pull up in the long drop off lane and inch his way to the front. When they would arrive at the entrance, Marlee would hop out of the car, walk to the door, pull it open, turn back towards the car, and give daddy The Marlee. Then she would casually go inside to meet her aide. Sometimes Dave could see her smile as he drove away.

19

The Selfies

Technology has come a long way since I was a kid. When I was growing up, rotary phones mounted on the kitchen wall serviced every member of a household. If you were lucky, your parents bought the extra-long phone cord. Then you would be able to talk in private by locking yourself in an adjacent closet or bathroom. In 1979, my father bought a car with a Citizens Band Radio, CB Radio for short. It was a mobile radio system that allowed people to communicate within a certain range. The CB Radio was popularized by the movie, Smokey and The Bandit. The movie was a favorite in our house as my mother loved Burt Reynolds. The CB Radio functioned like a modern-day chat room. You were able to converse with people you didn't know. It was a precursor to social media.

Marlee, like all kids, was fascinated with electronic gadgets. These days, children become acquainted with the digital world at an early age. So many of their toys, books, and games are designed to be interactive. Educational games from LeapFrog were a favorite in our house. Many of the products resembled an iPad or tablet and provided hands-on learning activities. Marlee's proficiency with LeapFrog products paved the way for her desire to use my personal laptop and iPad. She would log herself on to play games or listen to music. Although my parents had been at the

forefront of technology with the CB Radio, they had no
desire to pursue the digital world. The only devices they
possessed were flip phones and a Kindle. My mother had
a closet full of games, crayons, construction paper, books,
and coloring books for the kids to use when they came to
the house. When Marlee would spend time there, she would
spend hours coloring and flipping through all the books.
That all ended the day she found their Kindle. After much
persistence, my parents finally caved and let her use it. She
was able to access kid games, and my parents thought it was
harmless. Although my parents owned a Kindle, they were
leery of the Internet. They had never used a credit card over
the phone or computer to make online purchases. Packages
delivered to their home were a rarity.

A few days after one of Marlee's visits, the doorbell rang.
My mother answered to find UPS making a delivery to
their house. She checked with my father to see if he was
expecting any packages. He was not. There were three
boxes. The address was to my parent's house, but the
recipient's name said Marlee. When my mother opened
the large box, she found a comforter and bed sheets with
the characters from the Nickelodeon show Big Time Rush
imprinted on them. Along with the bedding, there was a
smaller package that had a pillow with the same theme.
The smallest box contained Willie Wonka Magic Gum.
Marlee was very much into Big Time Rush, and her favorite
movie at the time was Charlie and the Chocolate Factory.
In fact, days earlier I had to call poison control because she
drank Downy Fabric Softener hoping she would turn into a

blueberry like Wonka's character, Violet Beauregarde.

"How did she do this?" my mother exclaimed in a phone call to me. "How was she able to order these things and have them delivered to our house? Our credit card is not attached to this device."

"Mom," I said, "it's Marlee. She can do anything she puts her mind to."

In hindsight, the credit information must have been added to the Kindle at one time. The fact that she found the account information and figured out how to apply it to a purchase was terrifying. This was not the same as kids ordering things from Alexa and Echo. All they had to do was orally give a command. This had taken work on Marlee's part.

Marlee would also take advantage of an iPhone if left unattended. Remember the fish incident a couple of chapters back? Well, Marlee would once again leave her mark at their house. We had stopped over after attending a school event with Marlee. Stacy and Tom have a beautiful outdoor patio with comfy seats and an outdoor television. Tom invited Marlee to take his chair. He asked her what she would like to watch on television and changed the channel. Tom and Dave retreated into the house, while Stacy and I continued our conversation on the patio. Regrettably for Tom, he left his phone on the chair. He unintentionally created an opportunity for Marlee to gain access to it. This mistake would go unnoticed for days. It wasn't until a week later that Marlee's handiwork would be discovered. Tom had been meeting with a client who had asked to see a picture of his family. When he clicked on the photo gallery to retrieve one, over fifty pictures of Marlee popped up on his screen. She had managed to take the selfies while sitting in his chair. Tom got a chuckle out of seeing the pictures she had snapped. There was even the occasional photo of her giving The Marlee. What we learned was the camera on an IPhone was still accessible even though the phone was locked. But of course, Marlee already figured that out.

20

Sam

There is a quote floating around Pinterest that reads, "No home is complete without the pitter patter of kitty feet." I could not agree more. In 2008, we rescued two kitties from a shelter. Sam and Sal. Sal's hair was short, and his coat looked like a swirl of butterscotch. He was cautious around the children and preferred to keep to himself. Sam's hair was long with the same markings as a racoon. His coat was fluffy, and he had an enormous tail. He was content to hang out with the family all day. Sam and Marlee connected immediately. She became his person. It didn't take long after his arrival that he began inserting himself in her bedtime routine. Each night, Sam would wait outside the bathroom door for Marlee to finish showering. Sometimes he would sneak inside and climb into the shower with her. Once Marlee was done in the bathroom, Sam would climb into her bed. He would nestle under the covers, put his head on the pillow, and wait. Marlee would leap into bed and snuggle next to him.

He was there for story time, endless cups of water, and the switching of the lights from off to on and on to off. He would be bounced, smooched, smothered, and squeezed until Marlee fell asleep hugging him tight. And he wouldn't move. He would wait for Marlee to fall asleep. Once she was asleep, he would wiggle his way out from her grasp, and find a more comfortable space on the bed. He did this every night for eight years. The night before he died, he snuggled with me. Sam had an aneurism rupture the next day and he must have known he was going to be leaving us. He knew we would have to come up with a new bedtime routine and he was preparing us for the change. To this day Marlee talks about how much she misses her Sammy.

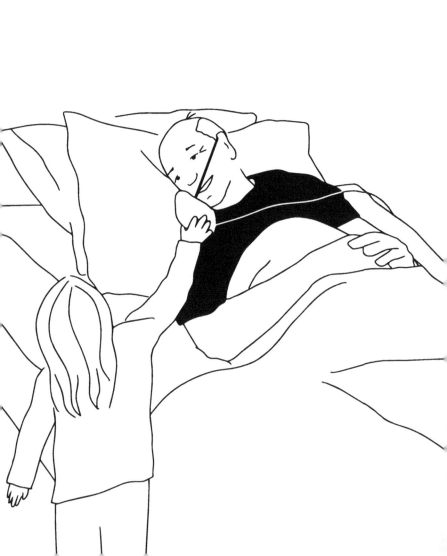

21

The Road Less Traveled

There is no question that some of the most dramatic instances that have taken place with Marlee have happened when Dave was in charge. Marlee can manipulate Dave. Like a lot of dads, Dave doesn't overreact to situations. He likes to wait it out, until there is no other option but to react. Whether it was with the runaway golf cart in the Bahamas or the vanishing goldfish at Stacy's house, Dave and Marlee have a knack for creating mayhem together. And they are quite good at it.

One of the first examples of this joint pandemonium occurred when Marlee was just five years old. Dave decided he was going to take Marlee for a ride to visit his mother. She only lived twenty minutes away, but the elevation was significantly higher. The snow had really piled up overnight and the back roads were slick.

It never occurred to me to say, "Stay on the main roads and don't drive up steep hills in areas with no cell reception." I just figured that common sense would prevail, especially in extreme weather conditions.

After visiting with his mom, Dave decided to take a detour on the way home. Marlee had fallen asleep in her car seat and he was curious how much snow had accumulated near the local ski club. The distance between the ski hill and

131

our house was about forty-five minutes. To get there, you needed to travel off the main road and up a very steep hill.

See where this is going?

When Dave reached the steep hill, he was only able to make it halfway up. Not one to give up so easily, he tried two more times to make it up the icy road. On the third try, he had almost reached the top before the wheels began to spin. Instead of regaining forward motion, the car began to go in reverse. Unable to gain control, the car slipped down the hill, plunging into a snowbank. Thankfully, neither Dave nor Marlee were hurt, but the impact was forceful enough to wake Marlee from her nap. Dave was unable to liberate the car from the snow. He would need to call for a tow. Unfortunately, the use of his phone was not an option as there was no cell reception in the area. Dave scooped Marlee from her car seat and began to walk to the only house in sight. It was white, and barely visible against the snowy backdrop.

Dave rang the doorbell and a petite, elderly lady answered the door. He explained what had happened and asked if he could use their phone to call for help.

"Oh my," the woman said, "please come in and warm up while you make the call." Looking at Marlee, she smiled and said, "Who is this little angel?"

Without giving Dave a chance to answer, Marlee bolted past the woman, running up the stairs. Now, as I have explained, Dave is not quick to react to situations. He stood there, unable to speak. He watched helplessly as Marlee bounded up the stairs in her winter attire. Snow was flying from her boots as she unzipped her coat and tossed her hat. She disappeared around the corner and the woman and Dave looked at each other. He offered an apology, but she told him not to worry.

With a wink she said, "There's nothing in this old house she can disturb."

They climbed the stairs together, but Marlee was nowhere to be found. The woman led Dave to another staircase in the back of the house. These stairs led to a room with an elderly man resting in a hospital bed. It was the woman's husband, who was very sick. He was hooked up to an oxygen tank. Usually the couple did not have visitors, but today would be different. Marlee was standing by the bed, lifting his oxygen mask, which revealed a smile.

The woman had tears in her eyes.

"My husband is very sick and can no longer leave our home, no one ever makes the long drive to see us. Your daughter made my husband smile. I believe she truly is an angel."

22

Where's Marlee

Over the years, I have become accustomed to family, friends, and neighbors letting me know the whereabouts of Marlee.

Doorbell Rings: "Mrs. Matto, Marlee is stuck in the Donella's pine tree. Way up towards the top."

Knock at the Door: "Lisa, Marlee climbed into the tree house and the trap door is open!"

Yell from Bedroom: "Mrs. Matto, Marlee's head is stuck in-between the mattress and the bedpost of Casey's loft. It's squishing her head."

Yell from Basement: "Mom, Marlee tipped the TV on my foot, I think both the TV and my foot are broken. Help!"

Yell from the Bathroom: "Mom, there are big clumps of hair all over the bathroom floor, I think Marlee cut her hair again."

Over the years I have learned not to panic when I get a special report regarding Marlee. Not long ago, though, I received a call from one of my neighbors that would cause me to become really frightened.

Phone Rings: "Hi Lisa, this is Laurie calling. Liam is on his way to the YMCA and noticed Marlee walking up a busy road. He didn't think much about it at first, but then decided to call me in case she is not supposed to be on that busy street. We wanted to let you know."

Before I could even register what was just said, my stomach turned to knots. Marlee had just returned home from spending three weeks at summer camp. Camp Ramapo is an amazing place for children with special needs. It is located in Rhinebeck, New York. It allows children who have an IEP as part of their regular school schedule to experience all the same fun activities that typical children enjoy while away at sleepaway camp. The facilities are beautiful and the ratio of counselors and staff to campers is one to one. The experience for Marlee was priceless. Along with participating in events and making new friends, it gave her a sense of independence. Maybe a little too much.

When Marlee returned from camp, we made a big deal of it. I would prepare her favorite meal and invite her grandparents over for dinner. She would hold court at the table and have everyone's undivided attention. Earlier in the day, Dave had picked Marlee up from camp by himself, as he had been in the area on business. Marlee emerged from the car and offered big hugs to all of us. After a brief description of camp life, she made her way down the street to see her friend Meaghan. Her visiting with Meaghan would give me time to start on her laundry, as well as dinner. I had just hung her comforter to dry when I received the call from Laurie.

My first thought was she couldn't possibly be walking up

Duguid Road. She was at Meaghan's house. It must be a mistake. I called Meaghan to verify Marlee was still there. Meaghan said that Marlee had left, and told her she was going back home.

The knots in my stomach began to tighten. Marlee had gone missing before, but she had never left the neighborhood.

I began to look for her myself and realized I was getting nowhere. Dave had gone to the YMCA to work out, so he was unreachable. Casey took matters into his hands and rounded up all the kids from the neighborhood. They began to mobilize in all directions. I called the police. Duguid was a busy street. It was a sequence of rolling hills, with many blind spots. In the time she was gone, I imagined horrible things happening to her. I was terrified she would be kidnapped or hit by a car.

My mother-in-law pulled into the driveway the same time the first police officer arrived. He wanted me to check the house again to be sure she wasn't hiding. I became very upset. I knew she was not in the house and did not want to waste time. My mother-in-law went back inside to search the house again. More police cars pulled up to the house, but there was still no sign of Marlee. To be honest, I had no idea our town had more than two or three officers. It was comforting to know they were out in full force looking for her.

Marlee was gone over an hour before a neighbor found her walking in a nearby neighborhood.

He pulled up next to her and said, "Marlee, everyone is looking for you! What are you doing?"

She replied by saying, "Who you?"

When Andy pulled up with Marlee in the car, I fell to my knees. I can honestly say I had never been so relieved or happy in my entire life. Once again, the neighborhood rallied behind Marlee and our family. I cannot thank Liam enough for realizing something was not right and calling his mother. That one small act could have been the difference in preventing a tragedy. Talk about following your gut, doing the right thing, and watching out for others. I cannot tell you the number of times I have thanked God for our neighbors. I am filled with immense gratitude for both them and our community.

23

Higher Ed

The move to the high school was exciting for Marlee and scary for me. How would she maneuver such a big building? How would she tackle schoolwork and homework? Would she fit in socially? Would she attend dances and football games? Would she have friends?

We were not the kind of parents who tried to arrange friendships with either of our children. For Casey, it was easy. He has been with the same posse of boys since grammar school. The group expanded when he went to high school. They are all still friends to this day.

But would Marlee ever have a squad? Would she find friends outside of the neighborhood that would last a lifetime, too?

A few weeks before Marlee started high school and Casey left for college, my mother passed away after being diagnosed with vasculitis. This is a condition that is typically not life threatening. The diagnosis came in May and she passed away in August. It was a devastating, tragic loss that profoundly affected us all.

When Marlee was born, at first my mother did not know how to cope with the sadness she felt for me and her only granddaughter. Let's face it, my parent's generation, as well as mine, did not have much interaction with people who had mental or physical disabilities. Most public schools hid these kids away from mainstream students in basement classrooms. Catholic and private schools were not even an option. They did not provide special education classes, nor did they incorporate modifications for learning into their curriculum. In the last 25 years, public and private schools have made great strides concerning the inclusion of students with disabilities. My mother had not been aware of the changes that occurred concerning special education. She didn't know that in our district, typical children sat side-by-side with children with disabilities. My mother was afraid kids would make fun of Marlee and treat her differently. The truth is, this generation has learned to accept inclusion in the classroom, as well as in the community. Over the years, I have had the pleasure of working with students who embrace all kinds of diversity. They have acute tolerance and acceptance regarding lifestyles and experiences that are different from their own. They are able to demonstrate acceptance and empathy to people who are different from themselves.

If you think about it, people like Marlee must demonstrate empathy all the time. Most people they interact with are different from them. Instead of distancing themselves from the typical world, they work hard to understand it and to fit in. Marlee doesn't worry about the past or the future. She is always focused on the present. She possesses clarity. An innate ability to tune in to someone else's emotions and gauge how they feel.

When we were ready to leave the hospital with Marlee, my mother was there to help. I had an adorable outfit picked out for her to wear. It included tiny pink tights, as well as a bright pink hair ribbon. The ribbon kept slipping down every time I tried to fasten it to her hair. She looked so cute. My mother was having a moment as we waited for the nurse to come with the wheelchair so we could be released from the hospital. She was holding Marlee and began to cry.

She looked up at me through her tears and said, "We always have to make sure she is dressed to the nines and has perfect hair."

I couldn't help but laugh. "No worries there, mom," I said. "She will definitely have the best of everything."

During the first few years both my parents would marvel at how she was able to attend pre-school and was included in birthday parties and playdates. They soon realized that the kids didn't see Marlee as being different. They saw her as their classmate and friend.

Freshman year was more of a learning curve for Marlee. She was getting to know the school, the kids, and her teachers. She was excited about the different clubs and activities that high school had to offer. By her sophomore year, she had landed the gig as manager for the freshman girls soccer team. It was a responsibility she took very seriously. She was there to pump up the girls at practice and cheer them on during games. Marlee instructed the team to refer to her as Manager Marlee. If they called her by any other name, she would immediately scold them. The team recognized Manager Marlee at their soccer banquet. It was an incredible feeling of pride to see Marlee interact with them and become a part of the team all on her own. Marlee had never shown an interest in playing or attending sports at school. It was through her desire to be with her peers that earned her a spot as the manager. One of the most joyful parts of parenting Marlee is watching her develop independence and choose her own path.

Marlee has stayed close with many of the girls who were part of that team. Many thanks go to the special education teachers who helped her to take advantage of these opportunities.

The teachers and aides who assisted Marlee throughout her school career were all an intricate part of her educational journey. Starting at the elementary level they would give her space and let her work through problems independently. Teacher aides are with their students in the hallway, the lunchroom, and the playground. They can assess many things about their students that teachers and administrators would not be able to identify.

1. How does the student do in social situations?

2. Do they have friends?

3. Can they maneuver the lunchroom, bathroom, playground, and corridors?

Marlee was fortunate to have been assigned qualified, competent, and caring aides. These professionals helped her through many situations over the years. They are a huge part of her success and they do not get enough credit. Because Marlee and her aides spent a lot of time together during the school day, they became very close. Over the years, some of Marlee's aides communicated to me how Marlee was able to help them when they were having a bad day. Mrs. Rett is one of those special people who was Marlee's aide for three years. In our district, students would have three or four different aides throughout the day. Mrs. Rett was the aide for Marlee during art class, as well as a couple other periods. Mrs. Rett was also one of Casey's best friend's mom. When I would see her at social functions, she would tell me funny stories about Marlee and how she was doing in school. One day she mentioned how Marlee had the ability to be closely in tune with people's feelings. I was curious what she meant and asked her to elaborate.

"Well," she said, "we were having a fun time in art class, when Marlee suddenly looked at me and said, 'what's wrong?' I was not acting any differently and class had been business as usual. When I asked Marlee what she meant she replied, 'you seem sad today.'"

Mrs. Rett had been surprised when Marlee said that because she was feeling down that day. She was surprised that Marlee was able to pick up on it.

"I remember thinking, "Wow, how does she know? For the rest of the period, Marlee made it her job to make me laugh. We were following along with what the class was doing and her interpretation of the lesson was hilarious. I immediately cheered up. We were both cracking up and I felt that we really connected after that. We built a trust in each other," she explained. "That is why we made such a great team."

Junior year saw Unified Sports implemented into the athletic program at the high school. Unified Sports partners typical and special needs kids together to compete in sports. The two sporting events Unified offered at our school were bowling and basketball. Marlee was all over it. Not so much for the actual competition, but for the comradery, and for the boys. She loved every aspect of participating on the team. She loved wearing her uniform on game day, riding the team bus, getting the snacks, and having a new bunch of friends. And Unified Sports attracted a huge following. Marlee would take her position on the basketball court and blow kisses to the crowd. She didn't give a darn if she ever touched the ball.

Unified Sports is the epitome of sportsmanship. Spectators cheer for athletes on both teams. I won't say it didn't matter if we lost, because, deep down, we always want to win. But I will say that we always left a Unified game feeling a little bit better about the world. Every school should have this program. There is a long waiting list of typical kids who want to participate in our district.

During one of the Unified basketball games, I overheard some of the high school girls talking about the junior prom. The prom has become an elaborate affair. When I attended my prom, I did my own hair and makeup. My date and I doubled with another couple. Pictures involved only the four of us, and my date drove us back and forth

in his father's Oldsmobile Supreme. Today, prepping
for prom is an all-day affair. Hair, makeup, and nails are
done by professionals. The perfect setting must be chosen
for a photoshoot that involves at least twenty couples.
After photos, the couples embark in limousines and are
chauffeured to the big dance. But, before any of this can take
place, there needs to be a prom proposal. A promposal is an
event in which great lengths are taken to invite someone to
attend the prom with you. The backdrop for such an event
has become more elaborate than most wedding proposals.

As I listened to the girls, I turned to Dave and said, "I don't
think Marlee is going to the prom."

One of the varsity lacrosse players overheard me and
said, "Mrs. Matto, I asked Marlee to the prom and she
turned me down."

I couldn't believe it. She never told me that she had been
asked to go to prom!

After the game I asked her, "Why didn't you tell me you
were invited to the prom?"

"Oh Mom, don't worry," she answered. "I am going to ask
Christian if he want to go. He's my good forever friend. We
will have lots of fun."

Christian was in fact one of her best buddies from the
neighborhood. He was a senior and was her friend
Meaghan's brother. She asked Christian without any
help from us. We didn't even know she had asked him
until his mom called and told us. We did pictures at our

147

house the night of the prom. Everyone in the family and the neighborhood showed up. Marlee looked stunning. They had a great time and were home before the clock struck midnight.

The local newspaper sends photographers to take prom and ball pictures for all of the area high schools. Marlee was in several of the candid photos the newspaper had printed. It was so much fun to see her and her classmates having such a great time. My favorite shot from the newspaper was of Marlee dancing in the middle of a circle, surrounded by friends. No caption needed, their smiles said it all.

24

Charlie

Charlie Poole was a classmate and friend to Marlee all throughout school. Charlie's family is the kind of family you would describe as the salt of the earth. If the Poole family came up in any conversation, folks would end the chat with the affirmation, good people. His brother was in Casey's grade and his sister was a couple years older than Casey. Charlie's parents were actively involved with their community, their church, and their kids. Great people! Charlie's mom, Lynda, was Marlee's occupational therapist in high school. Marlee never considered the time she spent with Lynda as classwork, because Lynda made every session so much fun.

When Charlie was 14 years old, he received a terminal diagnosis of a rare pediatric brain tumor known as DIPG. It was devastating news. Charlie and his family actively took on this diagnosis, exploring every option available. Charlie was involved in his medical care and attended many DIPG research conferences, as well as participated in several clinical trials. While fighting his own war against DIPG, he also became an advocate for kids with cancer. He assisted in developing programs in his own community to support and connect families battling this ugly disease.

Helping other kids while he fought cancer himself was not

surprising to anyone who knew him. That was Charlie. This boy, beautiful inside and out, ate lunch with Marlee all through middle school. Marlee was concerned about Charlie. When he was unable to attend school, she missed him. She would check in with Lynda about Charlie during occupational therapy. I was not sure if she understood the gravity of the situation. Charlie passed away the summer before his senior year. He was 17 years old. I was not sure how to share this sad news with Marlee. Little did I know, Marlee had been dealing with Charlie's illness in her own way. A few months after Charlie died, Lynda reached out to share with me a conversation she had with Marlee. She also told me that before Charlie died, Marlee had made a pillow for him during her summer school class. I emailed Lynda and asked if she would share this story with me again. I wanted to be sure to get it just right. She responded right away. Here is the email thread.

Hi Lynda,

I hope you and the family are well. Marlee misses you this year. I was wondering if you could help me with something. I have been writing a short book about Marlee and all of the unbelievable incidents she got herself and us into. I am also revealing her sensitive side and how she has been able to connect with people on a level most cannot. You told me about a beautiful interaction you had with Marlee where she asked if she could talk to you about Charlie. I was wondering if you could remind me about that and

*about when she gave Charlie the pillow she made for him.
I know they had lunch together and Marlee loved Charlie.
Would you mind if I included this in the book, as well as
honoring Charlie? I'm not sure if it will ever get anywhere
in the publishing world. It has been years in the making.
I have had an urge to write these last few weeks and
cannot explain the ease or the pace that has transpired.
I feel like I am being pushed and assisted by an energy
way beyond my own.*

*Please let me know what you think about including
Charlie, and if you would share those Marlee
moments with me again.*

Warmly,

Lisa

Hi Lisa,

*I love that you are writing. It has been so helpful for me as
well. I would be honored to tell you about the beautiful soul
your daughter is and would love you to include anything
you feel moved to about Charlie. She was often brought
up by Charlie over the years, with a smile, as he loved
her sass and humor.*

The story I told you was this....

*I returned to school a few weeks after Charlie died. It was
incredibly difficult to be back in the school without him
there. Many people would smile with sadness in their eyes,*

or say good to see you, or did not know what to say. I was walking down the hall in the morning, and Marlee saw me for the first time that school year. She came right over, and our conversation went like this:

"Hey! Mrs. Poole."

"Hi Marlee"

"I'm really sad about Charlie, that he died."

"Thank you Marlee, I'm sad too, thanks for saying that."

"Are you OK with me talking about this?"

"Yes, Marlee I love talking about him."

"I really liked him. He ate lunch with me. "

"I know, he used to tell me about the good times you had."

"Would it be OK if we got together and I told you stories about him?"

"I would love nothing more Marlee, thank you."

"OK see you later."

In that one brief conversation, she demonstrated perfectly how to support someone in grief. She looked me in the eye and acknowledged my sadness and hers, asked if I was OK talking about it, and wanted to sit with me and share about my person. That was such an incredible gift she gave me, such wisdom and kind heart when I needed it most.

She made a pillow in the summer program and sent it home

to Charlie. I know how hard it was for her to make that and how long it must have taken. Charlie did too, as that sunshine pillow sat on his bed every day until he died and is still there today. She and Charlie and Nick all used to eat lunch together at Wellwood. Charlie would be so happy to see the spectacular human Marlee has grown to be, but he knew it all along. Love, Lynda

Here is a photo of the pillow. I never knew it existed until Lynda shared the story with me. I love that the pattern Marlee chose for the pillow was the sun. I love that the pillow radiates warmth. A smiling sun with a cool pair of sunglasses. It is how I picture Charlie, smiling down on his beautiful family, friends, and community, bringing warmth and hope to all battling cancer, especially children. I picture him as one of Marlee's guardian angels. Guiding her steps. Cheering her on. And smiling.

25

Grace

The first entry of the Merriam-Webster definition for Grace is unmerited divine assistance given to humans for their regeneration or sanctification. A few lines down the description reads, disposition to or an act or instance of kindness, courtesy, or clemency.

Because Marlee lives in the present, she is free of so many of the burdens that weigh the rest of us down. She does not try to put her life in any particular order, but rather accepts her order as perfection. She goes with the flow. She does not stay sad or angry when disappointed by people or situations. She quickly moves on and always forgives. Marlee lives her life in a state of grace. She has clarity about what is important in life. She is connected to people and the earth to a far greater level then most humans will ever reach. Giving her the middle name Grace, in honor of my friend's mother, has taken on a much bigger meaning to me. She not only has been able to show grace to others, she has instinctively attracted or invited the grace of others into her life.

The summer before senior year began, Marlee informed me that her friend Grace was coming to pick her up. I had never heard Marlee mention a Grace before. I did not know her last name or where she lived. Marlee did not have access to a phone. She had an Instagram account on her iPad and, unbeknownst to me, was communicating with friends using direct messaging. I didn't know what to do. Should I let her get in the car with a school friend I did not know? I called my friend Stacy and asked her what I should do. Her daughter Marley was also a senior. Her response was an immediate YES. She went on to say that if Marlee did not have Down syndrome, I wouldn't question a female friend coming to pick her up on a Saturday afternoon. After thinking about it, I knew she was right. Grace picked up Marlee that afternoon. I let Marlee go. Grace did not grow up in Fayetteville and was new to the area. I was nervous because I didn't know anything about her or her family. I was taking a leap of faith by letting her go, but I soon realized that Grace embodied all the goodness her name implied.

Grace would call Marlee and invite her to attend school and sporting events with her and other friends. Previously, for any social event at school, we would have to arrange for an aide to be with her at the function. We would also drive and pick her up. There was never a gaggle of giggling girls who accompanied her. Marlee was so excited to go to these events with Grace. Grace's demeanor was always calm and patient. She had a beauty that went beyond physical features. Her gentleness was evident to everyone, especially Marlee. She unknowingly gifted Marlee with freedom and independence. Grace picked Marlee up for the homecoming football game, as well as every dance at school that year.

Marlee also became very close with some of her friends

from Unified Sports. She put together her own squad, which included her two new besties, Hannah and Jess. Their family has embraced Marlee like one of their own. She is on the phone with them all day long. Her first sleepover with friends was at their house. The girls are constantly making plans to do something with Marlee. We love them dearly!

Senior year proved to be a wonderful experience for Marlee. It also quelled my fears about whether she would have a squad, ride in a car with friends, and be part of those monumental experiences in high school. I am not going to tell you it was always smooth sailing, because it was not. I will tell you that her squad allows room for the occasional meltdown and stubbornness that Marlee can display. They work just as hard as we do to keep Marlee on track.

Marlee attended her senior ball with her squad. She had a graduation party that rocked the block, and she graduated with her class. She participated in the ceremony without the assistance of a teacher's aide. The students had to arrive at the arena ahead of time for one last rehearsal. I was planning on taking her up early when Grace called and offered to give her a ride. Marlee was smiling from ear to ear. She called from the top of the stairs, "Mom, can I go to graduation with Grace?" "Of course, you can," I said.

And off she went. She climbed into the car with Grace, clutching her cap and her gown. She looked out the window and waved goodbye. It was a moment I never imagined would happen, and a moment I never will forget.

Epilogue: To Marlee from Hannah

Dear Marlee,

For school I have to write a letter to someone that has lifted me up in life and influenced me as a person so I chose you. Our friendship started through the phone, when you somehow got my snapchat and started talking to me. I had done Unified the year before but you would not talk to me because I was a girl. Texting soon led to us hanging out for the first time two summers ago, right before school started. From then on I had a feeling that we would be spending a lot more time together. We now hang out all of the time, text, call, and you are one of my bestest friends- you even took me to the ball :)

You have lifted me up as a person because you have taught me so many things since I became your friend. You have taught me how to be a good friend, how to be more patient, and definitely how to be more outgoing. You are the most outgoing person I know, especially when it comes to boys. When I am with you, we are always the center of attention. I love this about you and it makes you such a fun person to be around. You have helped me through high school because you have shown me that it is okay to be the center of attention and that I should not care what people think about me. Before I met you I was so shy and had a hard time talking to new people and adults. After I spent some time with you (and your family), everything changed. I feel so much more confident in social situations and I am much more prepared for a life beyond high school. When we both leave for college, I hope that we can see each other on breaks because I am going to miss you so much. Maybe I will come to your house and eat your mom's pizza!!!

Miss Marlee Matto, you have been by my side for the past two years and it has made me 100 times happier. You have always been able to put a smile on my face. Thank you for coming to all of my soccer games and cheering me on and thank you for making me the person I am today. I would not be where I am today without you.

Love, Hannah

To be continued...

Jess & Marlee

Marlee, Hannah, and Adam at the
Unified Sports Banquet

Universal Studio's Diagon Alley
2018

Marlee making a basket
at her Unified game

Grace and Marlee at the
Homecoming Football Game

Marlee with her senior ball group

Marlee dancing at the prom

Marlee and Christian at the prom.
Ben behind Marlee

Manager Marlee

Marlee and Sam the cat

Marlee Voting in the
2020 Presidential Election

Marlee and Sam at the
Homecoming Football Game

Senior night with Dad and Casey

Marlee at Graduation

Matto Party of 4